SCHOLASTIC

NO FUSS

MATHS
PHOTOCOPIABLES
AGES 7-11

D1343572

LEVELS
3-5

- Levelled and linked to the curriculum

- Stand-alone photocopiable activities

- Ideal for mixed-age classes

Compiled by Roger Smith

CONTRIBUTORS

Text © **Sally Abbey, Trevor Easterbrook and Lynne Pointer**: 17, 18, 19, 22, 23, 25, 26, 27, 28, 29, 33, 41, 44, 51, 56, 57, 58, 62, 71, 72, 73, 74, 75, 76, 78, 89, 96, 102, 103, 104, 105, 106, 107, 108

Text © **Catherine Musto and Marion Cranmer**: 15, 16, 20, 21, 30, 31, 32, 34, 38, 39, 40, 42, 43, 45, 46, 47, 50, 59, 60, 61, 67, 69, 70, 79, 80, 81, 87, 88, 94, 95, 98, 99, 100, 101, 109, 110, 111, 112, 113, 114, 120, 121

Text © **John Davis and Sonia Tibbatts**: 24, 35, 36, 37, 48, 49, 52, 53, 54, 55, 63, 64, 65, 66, 68, 82, 83, 84, 85, 86, 90, 91, 92, 93, 97

Text © **Leonie McKinnon**: 77, 115, 116, 117, 118, 119, 122, 123, 124, 125, 126, 127

CONSULTANT EDITOR

Roger Smith

ASSISTANT EDITOR

Wendy Tse

DESIGNERS

Lapiz Digital

COVER DESIGN

Anna Oliwa

ILLUSTRATORS

Illustration © **Debbie Clark**: 17, 18, 19, 22, 23, 25, 26, 27, 28, 29, 33, 41, 44, 51, 56, 57, 58, 62, 71, 72, 73, 74, 75, 76, 78, 89

Illustration © **Caroline Ewen**: 77, 115, 116, 117, 118, 119, 122, 123, 124, 125, 126, 127

Illustration © **Gloria**: 15, 16, 21, 30, 31, 34, 38, 39, 42, 46, 50, 60, 61, 67, 69, 79, 81, 87, 94, 99, 100, 101, 111, 114, 120, 121

Illustration © **Hilary McElderry**: 32, 43, 45, 47, 59, 70, 88, 95, 109, 110, 112

Illustration © **Sarah Rushton**: 96, 102, 103, 104, 105, 106, 107, 108

Illustration © **Liz Thomas**: 24, 36, 48, 52, 53, 54, 55, 63, 65, 66, 68, 82, 83, 84, 85, 86, 90, 91, 97

Text and illustration copyright in individual pages as per acknowledgements.
Compilation © 2006 Scholastic Ltd

Every effort has been made to trace all the copyright owners of material but there were a few cases where an author or illustrator was untraceable. Scholastic will be happy to correct any omissions in future printings.

Published by Scholastic Ltd

Book End
Range Road
Witney
Oxfordshire
OX29 0YD

www.scholastic.co.uk

Designed using Adobe InDesign

Printed by Bell & Bain Ltd, Glasgow

9   0 1 2 3 4 5

British Library Cataloguing-in-Publication Data

A catalogue record for this book is available from the British Library.

ISBN 0-439-96551-9

ISBN 978-0439-96551-4

Extracts from the National Numeracy Strategy reproduced under the terms of HMSO Guidance Note 8. © Crown copyright.

Reproduction of coins by permission of The Royal Mint © Crown copyright.

Photocopiable pages and original teachers' notes first published in *Fractions and decimals, Shape and space in two dimensions* and *Working with numbers up to 200* (all first published 1994) from the Essentials for Maths series, and *Exploring shape and space* (1996), *Maths* (1992), *Maths puzzles* (1994) and *Measurement skills* (1996) from the Teacher Timesavers series.

All rights reserved. This book is sold subject to the condition that it shall not, by way of trade or otherwise, be lent, hired out or otherwise circulated without the publisher's prior consent in any form of binding or cover other than that in which it is published and without a similar condition, including this condition, being imposed upon the subsequent purchaser.

No part of this publication may be reproduced, stored in a retrieval system, or transmitted, in any form or by any means, electronic, mechanical, photocopying, recording or otherwise, without the prior permission of the publisher. This book remains copyright, although permission is granted to copy pages where indicated for classroom distribution and use only in the school which has purchased the book, or by the teacher who has purchased the book, and in accordance with the CLA licensing agreement. Photocopying permission is given only for purchasers and not for borrowers of books from any lending service.

Mixed Sources
Product group from well-managed forests and other controlled sources
www.fsc.org Cert no. TT-COC-002769
© 1996 Forest Stewardship Council

www.scholastic.co.uk

Great Job

CONTENTS

CONTENTS

INTRODUCTION

The main purpose of this book is to provide teachers with a set of easy-to-use, varied and stimulating activities, which are linked to the National Numeracy Strategy for England and the Scottish National Guidelines for Mathematics 5-14. These activities will not only provide back-up learning materials for individuals, pairs and groups but can also be used as extension work to support other resources and, because they are graded in levels, be used as part of any assessment process.

Using a wide range of resources is essential to meaningful learning in mathematics. By using these activities you will be able to:

- introduce new skills and concepts
- encourage children to practise skills in the manipulation of numbers and symbols
- consolidate and reinforce a mathematical concept
- demonstrate the possibility of using ideas and information in a new situation
- add elements of flexibility to your maths teaching
- gain some indication of the children's current level of attainment.

The various sections of the National Numeracy Strategy, such as Calculations and Measures, shape and space, and of the Scottish National Guidelines for Mathematics 5-14, such as Information handling and Shape, position and movement, exist as discrete elements but there is also some overlap.

This is also the case with some of the activities in this book, which may be placed in one section but could equally be used in another. It is worth familiarising yourself with them. Each activity has also been allocated a level of difficulty but you will know your children and what they are or are not capable of completing; it is possible that some of the levels and activities can be adjusted to fit individuals or groups.

The activities should not just be given to children to complete on their own. It is important that there are discussions between the teacher and children at all stages. It is also useful to extend activities, where possible, and explore new avenues suggested by the children. All the activities can be completed using resources and equipment which are either readily available in the classroom or easily collected. Where it is appropriate children should be encouraged to use practical apparatus and calculators and computers.

Finally, all the activities should be interesting and encourage children to both learn the maths they need to know and to enjoy it. For some children maths can be a challenge and there are activities here that will help them rise to the challenge. For some children maths is an exciting adventure where they always want to learn more so at the end of most of the activities there are suggestions for further work, which should mean that even in the busiest and most mixed-ability classroom there should be something for everyone.

Page	Activity	Objective	Teachers' notes	National Numeracy Strategy links	Scottish Curriculum links	KS2 Levels
page 15	Looking for patterns	To count on and back following a number pattern.	The first two sequences count on in twos and fives, respectively, but the third sequence is slightly more difficult. The children work out that the sequence involves counting back in nines. When the children are making up their own sequences, they should only count on in twos, threes, fives or tens.	Counting, properties of numbers and number sequences: Describe and extend number sequences.	Number, money and measurement – Level A	AT2 Level 2/3
page 16	Mr Mystery Maker	To compare and order numbers.	Encourage the children to be adventurous and perhaps to try more than one operation when devising their own 'spells'.	Counting, properties of numbers and number sequences: Describe and extend number sequences. Reasoning about numbers or shapes: Solve mathematical puzzles by recognising simple patterns and relationships.	Number, money and measurement – Level A	AT2 Level 2/3
page 17	Tile designs	To begin to understand how to divide a 'whole' into various fractions.	The children should have time to look at each other's solutions, to reinforce that the value of a fraction is not changed by the parts being grouped together or separated. Two children might colour in a quarter of the shape blue but they might have chosen to colour in completely different parts.	Fractions: Recognise simple fractions of a whole.	Number, money and measurement – Level A/B	AT2 Level 2/3
pages 18 and 19	Fraction flags – 1 and 2	To begin to understand how to divide a 'whole' into various fractions.	The children should have time to look at each other's solutions. It may be useful to enlarge both pages to A3 size.	Fractions: Recognise simple fractions of a whole.	Number, money and measurement – Level A/B	AT2 Level 2/3
page 20	Bigger and bigger	To begin to organise numbers up to 10,000 and to multiply by 10 and 100.	Children could use calculators when making up their own missing number table. If appropriate, introduce the use of decimals.	Place value: Demonstrate understanding of multiplying a whole number by 10, 100 and 1000.	Number, money and measurement – Level B/C	AT2 Level 3
page 21	New uniforms	To understand fractions of a whole.	The children could start by making symmetrical designs and then more creative ones. This activity could be made more difficult by using fractions such as 2/3, 3/8, 5/8, and so on.	Fractions and decimals: Use fraction notation and recognise simple fractions that are several parts of a whole.	Number, money and measurement – Level B/C	AT2 Level 3
page 22	Slices of pie	To understand fractions of a whole.	Pairing children appropriately is essential for this game. They could make a version of this game using different fractions, such as sixths, thirds and halves.	Fractions and decimals: Use fraction notation and recognise simple fractions that are several parts of a whole.	Number, money and measurement – Level B/C	AT2 Level 3
page 23	Corner numbers	To begin to order fractions and understand decimal notation.	It might be useful to use calculators for some of this activity. The missing numbers may be given as fractions or decimals. The children could explore which ones can be solved in which way and why.	Fractions and decimals: Use fraction notation and recognise simple fractions that are several parts of a whole and mixed numbers.	Number, money and measurement – Level C	AT2 Level 3/4
page 24	Function mazes	To extend number sequences using specific rules.	This is really a starter activity for the children to make up more complex function mazes using three functions and two- and three-digit numbers. The children could give a list of outputs only for their friends to try, in order to develop an understanding of inverse operations. Extend this activity by asking the children to make a table showing their inputs and outputs for each function maze. Is there a pattern if the inputs are a series of consecutive numbers?	Properties of numbers and number sequences: Recognise and extend number sequences.	Number, money and measurement – Level C	AT2 Level 3/4
page 25	Just two	To use and understand decimal notation.	Different solutions are possible so a pair or group could be asked to find more than one solution for each of the numbers in the grid.	Fractions and decimals: Use decimal notation for tenths.	Number, money and measurement – Level C/D	AT2 Level 3/4
page 26	Box the digits	To understand decimal notation and know what each digit represents.	There are many different solutions to the first three puzzles so children should be encouraged to compare their answers and to check that they have found all the possible solutions.	Fractions and decimals: Use decimal notation for tenths and hundredths.	Number, money and measurement – Level C/D	AT2 Level 3/4

SCHOLASTIC
www.scholastic.co.uk

Page	Activity	Objective	Teachers' notes	National Numeracy Strategy links	Scottish Curriculum links	KS2 Levels
pages 27 and 28	Bingo and Bingo cards	To order given sets of digits and know what each digit represents.	Discuss with the children whether there are ways of using the numbers systematically and strategically.	Making decisions: Choose and use appropriate number operations and appropriate ways of calculating to solve problems.	Number, money and measurement – Level C/D	AT2 Level 3/4
page 29	Four ways	Use the vocabulary of comparing and ordering numbers.	This activity may benefit from a tight time limit, or to two ways for less able children.	Making decisions: Choose and use appropriate number operations and appropriate ways of calculating to solve problems.	Number, money and measurement – Level C/D	AT2 Level 3/4
page 30	Decimal numbers	To order a mixed set of decimal numbers.	Use thin card for the numbers. If it is not possible to make the two piles equal, then the children should try to make them as close as possible.	Fractions and decimals: Use decimal notation for tenths and hundredths.	Number, money and measurement – Level D/E	AT2 Level 4/5
page 31	Jolly jumpers	To use a fraction as an operator to find fractions of quantities.	This helps children to realise that the sale item with the greatest reduction may not be the cheapest.	Fractions and decimals: Relate fractions to division and solve simple problems involving ratio and proportion.	Number, money and measurement – Level D/E	AT2 Level 5
page 32	Decimal fun!	To create decimal fractions lying between two others.	It is important that calculators are available for this activity. This activity develops an appreciation of what happens when decimal numbers are divided.	Fractions and decimals: Give a decimal fraction lying between two others.	Number, money and measurement – Level D/E	AT2 Level 5
page 33	Which would you rather have?	To recognise relationships between fractions.	Children need to discuss their answers with a partner. They should first try to arrive at the largest grand total they can. Next they need to take some time to decide on which choices to change to arrive nearer to the target total of 300. They should then discuss which is the closest to the target of 300.	Fractions and decimals: Relate fraction to division.	Number, money and measurement – Level D	AT2 Level 4
page 34	Making a tables game	To understand simple multiplication.	Remind the children that each product is only recorded once. Keep lots of spare copies of this page, or get the children to draw the table themselves if they remember the rules, as it is useful to use several times.	Rapid recall of multiplication facts: Know by heart multiplication facts for the 2 and 5 times-tables and begin to know the 3 and 4 times-tables.	Number, money and measurement – Level B	AT2 Level 2/3
page 35	Best guess	To add and subtract two-digit numbers.	Make sure that the children do estimate their answers first and they 'round' numbers up or down to estimate. The sums can be changed before the page is copied to match the children's ability.	Understanding addition and subtraction: Extend understanding of the operations of addition and subtraction.	Number, money and measurement – Level A/B	AT2 Level 3
page 36	Number chains	To develop rapid addition of single and two digit numbers.	Encourage the children to develop their own number chains and to try them out with friends.	Understanding addition and subtraction: Extend understanding of the operation of addition.	Number, money and measurement – Level A/B	AT2 Level 3
page 37	Crafty corners	To develop further understanding of multiplication and to use a calculator.	This includes quite difficult multiplication so it is important that children are allowed to use calculators. Encourage them to try their own squares.	Checking results of calculations: Check with an equivalent calculation.	Number, money and measurement – Level A/B	AT2 Level 3
page 38	Which number?	To extend the children's knowledge of multiplication.	This activity is best completed in pairs or even small groups. It will reinforce the idea that tables do not stop at 10 x 10. The children should find a suitable way of recording their findings.	Understanding multiplication and division: Extend understanding of the operations of multiplication.	Number, money and measurement – Level C	AT2 Level 3/4
page 39	Possible products	To extend the children's knowledge of multiplication.	It is important to sort and classify results. Discussion and adult support may be needed to see whether all possible results have been obtained.	Understanding multiplication and division: Extend understanding of the operations of multiplication.	Number, money and measurement – Level C	AT2 Level 3/4
page 40	Matching the pairs	To extend the children's knowledge of multiplication.	A calculator may be helpful to check results. The children could explore equivalencies using other operations.	Understanding multiplication and division: Extend understanding of the operations of multiplication.	Number, money and measurement – Level C	AT2 Level 3/4

Page	Activity	Objective	Teachers' notes	National Numeracy Strategy links	Scottish Curriculum links	KS2 Levels
page 41	In between	To encourage paper and pencil procedures to explain calculations.	Number lines might be useful for this activity.	Pencil and paper procedures: Develop and refine written methods.	Number, money and measurement – Level C	AT2 Level 3/4
page 42	Stock check	To use informal pencil and paper procedures and extend knowledge of the four operations.	It would be possible to use this activity to develop calculator skills. The children could develop this activity by writing an order so that all items are in stock for the next month, based on the sales figures given being the average for a week.	Making decisions: Choose and use appropriate number operations and appropriate ways of calculating to solve problems.	Number, money and measurement – Level C/D	AT2 Level 3/4
page 43	Can you calculate?	To use the calculator to complete operations and to correct results.	Encourage the children to estimate the answer – by using pencil and paper if appropriate – before doing the calculation.	Checking results of calculations: Check with the inverse operation when using a calculator.	Number, money and measurement – Level C/D	AT2 Level 4
page 44	Twenty	To improve mental strategies involving decimal addition.	Discussing the process and the answers is an important part of this activity.	Mental calculation strategies (+ and –): Add 3 or 4 small numbers.	Number, money and measurement – Level C/D	AT2 Level 3/4
page 45	Use your head	To use paper and pencil methods for multiplication and division.	Sharing their methods with a partner will show children that there are different ways of calculating answers.	Pencil and paper procedures (× and ÷): Approximate first and use informal pencil and paper methods to record multiplications and division.	Number, money and measurement – Level D	AT2 Level 4
page 46	Make it big	To use paper and pencil methods for multiplication and division.	The number of digits used could be limited on increased depending on the children's ability. It is important that the children explain or generalise about their discoveries, and discuss their methods with a partner.	Pencil and paper procedures (× and ÷): Approximate first and use informal pencil and paper methods to record multiplications and division.	Number, money and measurement – Level D/E	AT2 Level 4/5
page 47	Square numbers	To recognise and calculate square numbers up to 10 × 10.	Encourage the children to discuss the relationships between the numbers.	Properties of numbers and number sequences: Recognise and extend number sequences.	Number, money and measurement – Level D/E	AT2 Level 4/5
page 48	Square-eyed	To recognise and calculate square numbers up to 10 × 10.	Allow the children to try this using paper and pencil calculations and then give them a calculator. This activity encourages children to think about square numbers and to improve their estimating skills.	Properties of numbers and number sequences: Recognise and extend number sequences.	Number, money and measurement – Level D/E	AT2 Level 4/5
page 49	Which key?	To use a calculator effectively.	The children should be encouraged to make reasoned estimates first before using the calculator. Answers: 1) ÷, ×; 2) –, ×; 3) +, ÷; 4) –, +; 5) ×, ÷; 6) –, ×; 7) +, ÷; 8) ÷, –; 9) ×, –; 10) –, ÷; 11) ÷, ×; 12) –, ÷.	Using a calculator: Develop calculator skills and use a calculator effectively.	Number, money and measurement – Level D/E	AT2 Level 4/5
page 50	Rolling dice	To use appropriate ways of finding answers to multiplication problems.	Some children may need support to work systematically. Ensure that they explore all possible solutions – they may need help in devising a table to record this.	Reasoning about numbers or shapes: Investigate statements about familiar numbers.	Problem-solving and enquiry – Level A/B	AT1 Level 4/5
page 51	Dartboards	To use appropriate ways to find answers about addition.	Ask questions such as *How can you be sure that it is the largest or smallest number?* to encourage systematic working and checking results. The children may choose the same or a different rule for the shaded ring of the dartboard, which will affect their answers.	Reasoning about numbers or shapes: Investigate statements about familiar numbers.	Problem-solving and enquiry – Level A/B	AT1 Level 2/3
page 52	Mystery number crossword	To choose the appropriate operation to solve a word problem.	Children who have language but not mathematical difficulties may need help with this activity. This gives the children practice in writing number names.	Making decisions: Choose and use appropriate operations to solve word problems.	Problem-solving and enquiry – Level A/B	AT1 Level 2/3
page 53	Times bingo	To investigate problems associated with familiar numbers.	Encourage the children to play this game several times and to invent their own bingo card.	Reasoning about numbers or shapes: Investigate statements about familiar numbers.	Problem-solving and enquiry – Level A/B	AT1 Level 3

■SCHOLASTIC
www.scholastic.co.uk

Page	Activity	Objective	Teachers' notes	National Numeracy Strategy links	Scottish Curriculum links	KS2 Levels
page 54	Hangmaths	To solve a mathematical problem involving addition.	Children need to be able to use a paper and pencil method of adding two- and three-digit numbers – it will help if they try this activity with two-digit numbers first.	Reasoning about numbers and shapes: Solve mathematical problems or puzzles. Pencil and paper procedures: Develop and refine written methods.	Problem-solving and enquiry – Level C	ATI Level 3/4
page 55	Sequences	To solve problems involving sequences of numbers.	You might have to select which of the sequences to do because some of the later ones are difficult. The children could make up some of their own to try with a friend. Rules for the sequences: 1) Add 5; 2) Subtract 7; 3) Add 3, add 4; 4) Subtract 5, subtract 2; 5) Add a quarter; 6) Add 1; 7) Subtract three-quarters; 8) Add two-tenths, add four tenths; 9) Add 0.2; 10) Subtract 0.5; 11) Subtract 0.25; 12) Add 0.12.	Properties of numbers and number sequences: Recognise and extend number sequences.	Problem-solving and enquiry – Level C	ATI Level 3/4
page 56	1,2,3,4	To solve mathematical problems involving all four operations.	This activity uses a calculator but could be completed without one. Encourage the children to use all four operations, and some children may use squared numbers, brackets and the √function.	Reasoning about numbers and shapes: Solve mathematical problems and puzzles.	Problem-solving and enquiry – Level C	ATI Level 3/4
page 57	Press here	To solve mathematical problems involving all four operations.	This activity uses a calculator but could be completed without one. It explores number sentences with mixed operations.	Reasoning about numbers and shapes: Solve mathematical problems or puzzles.	Problem-solving and enquiry – Level C	ATI Level 3/4
page 58	Two 2s	To solve mathematical problems involving all four operations.	It is possible to change the numbers to larger ones – but this activity is deceptively hard as it is.	Reasoning about numbers and shapes: Solve mathematical problems or puzzles.	Problem-solving and enquiry – Level C	ATI Level 3/4
page 59	Starting numbers	To choose and use appropriate strategies.	Children will have to use mental strategies involving all four operations.	Making decisions: Choose and use appropriate number operations and appropriate ways of calculating to solve problems.	Problem-solving and enquiry – Level C/D	ATI Level 4
page 60	How close can you get?	To choose and use appropriate strategies.	This activity encourages children to handle numbers to several decimal places and to make judgements about their closeness. They should record each attempt to compare nearness to 100. A calculator should be used after completing the activity to see if even closer answers are possible.	Making decisions: Choose and use appropriate number operations and appropriate ways of calculating to solve problems.	Problem-solving and enquiry – Level C/D	ATI Level 3/4
page 61	Television times	To choose and use appropriate strategies.	There should be opportunities for children to justify their answers and to appreciate the influence of events, such as a general election or a war.	Making decisions: Choose and use appropriate number operations and appropriate ways of calculating to solve problems.	Problem-solving and enquiry – Level C/D	ATI Level 4
page 62	Ordering equipment	To choose and use appropriate strategies.	There should be opportunities to discuss methods and answers. Talk about other situations where rounding up will also be needed.	Making decisions: Choose and use appropriate number operations and appropriate ways of calculating to solve problems.	Problem-solving and enquiry – Level C/D	ATI Level 3/4
page 63	Table repeats	To recognise and explain a number pattern.	Children could try linking the 9 times-table to the times-tables on the page. They could also explore any links between the 2, 4 and 8 times-tables, or the 5 and 10 times-tables.	Properties of numbers and number sequences: Recognise and extend number sequences.	Problem-solving and enquiry – Level D	ATI Level 4
page 64	Three jumps to 100	To recognise and explain a number pattern.	This can be a very long activity and can be completed over a period of time. It is important to note that only single digits can be used for the operations. Encourage the children to vary the use of the four signs as much as possible.	Making decisions: Choose and use appropriate number operations and appropriate ways of calculating to solve problems.	Problem-solving and enquiry – Level D	ATI Level 4

SCHOLASTIC
www.scholastic.co.uk

Page	Activity	Objective	Teacher's notes	National Numeracy Strategy links	Scottish Curriculum links	KS2 Levels
page 65	Integers	To recognise and explain a number pattern.	Children need to understand negative numbers before starting this activity. Answers: 1) 3; 2) -3; 3) 1, 4, 7; 4) 7°C; 5) 8°C; 6) 2°C.	Place value, ordering and rounding: Find the difference between a positive and negative integer.	Problem-solving and enquiry – Level E	AT1 Level 5
page 66	Fibonacci	To recognise and explain a number pattern.	This is an activity that needs lots of time and discussion. This number sequence can be easily continued to allow children to work with much larger numbers. They can look at odd and even numbers, and the differences between consecutive numbers. This number sequence also occurs in the natural world, for example in the development of spirals such as snails' shells.	Properties of numbers and number sequences: Recognise and extend number sequences.	Problem-solving and enquiry – Level E	AT1 Level 5
page 67	The birthday party	To solve problems associated with money.	Include the party giver as well as the guests when working out how many of each item to buy. Prices should be adjusted to suit the children's level of ability.	Problems involving 'real life', money or measures: Solve problems involving money in real life by finding totals and giving change.	Number, money and measurement – Level B/C	AT2 Level 3
page 68	Book fair	To solve problems associated with money.	Prices could be adjusted to suit ability and calculators could be used. Answers: Joanne could buy Creepy Tales and Short Stories 1 or 2; Sam could buy, for example, Short Stories 1, Puzzle Book, Sticker Book 1 or 2 and Tree Spotter; 36p.	Problems involving 'real life', money or measures: Solve problems involving money in real life by finding totals and giving change.	Number, money and measurement – Level B/C	AT2 Level 3
page 69	Lose or gain!	To solve problems associated with money.	Make a selection of coins available and a number line up to 100 might also be useful because, although it is a money problem, this activity is also about rounding numbers under 100.	Problems involving 'real life', money or measures: Solve problems involving money in real life by finding totals and giving change.	Number, money and measurement – Level B	AT2 Level 3
page 70	Link amounts	To solve problems associated with money.	Children need to be familiar with the different ways of recording money, including on a calculator where there will be no £ sign.	Problems involving 'real life', money or measures: Solve problems involving money in real life by finding totals and giving change.	Number, money and measurement – Level B	AT2 Level 3
page 71	Coin corners	To use addition to solve similar money problems.	Remind the children before they start that some of the amounts are impossible because of the limited set.	Problems involving 'real life', money or measures: Use all four operations to solve problems involving money.	Number, money and measurement – Level C	AT2 Level 3/4
page 72	Christmas cards	To use addition to solve similar money problems.	The words 'assortment' and 'selection' may need to be explained. The children's choices might depend on aesthetic appeal as well as price. They do not have to spend exactly £2.	Problems involving 'real life', money or measures: Use all four operations to solve problems involving money.	Number, money and measurement – Level C	AT2 Level 3/4
page 73	Bus conductor	To use addition to solve similar money problems.	This could be modified by insisting that the change has to be in the smallest number of coins.	Problems involving 'real life', money or measures: Use all four operations to solve problems involving money.	Number, money and measurement – Level C	AT2 Level 3/4
pages 74, 75 and 76	Lunch time and Lunch-time playing cards 1 and 2	To choose operations to solve 'real life' money problems.	This activity may take longer than you think and children will need scrap paper to keep track of the cost of their meals.	Problems involving 'real life', money or measures: Use all four operations to solve problems involving money.	Problem-solving and enquiry – Level C/D	AT2 Level 3/4
page 77	Babysitting	To choose operations to solve 'real life' money problems.	The children may need reminding of the concept of 'rounding up'. Extra paper will be needed for the working out. Answers for the table (client / actual time / rounded up time / money earned): Hunter / 3.30 / 3.30 / £8.50; Stephens / 5.15 / 5.15 / £13.00; MacLeod / 2.52 / 3 / £7.50; Jones / 4 / 4 / £10.00; Hunter / 6.21 / 6.30 / £16.00; Hunter / 11.18 / 11.30 / £28.50; MacLeod / 1.14 / 1.15 / £3.00; Jones / 6.02 / 6.15 / £15.50; Jones / 6.40 / 6.45 / £16.50; Hunter / 6.06 / 6.15 / £15.50. Total earnings: £134.00 (Hunter – £68.50; Stephens – £13.00; MacLeod – £10.50; Jones – £42.00. Best client: Hunter.	Problems involving 'real life', money or measures: Use all four operations to solve problems involving money.	Problem-solving and enquiry – Level C/D	AT2 Level 4

SCHOLASTIC
www.scholastic.co.uk

Page	Activity	Objective	Teachers' notes	National Numeracy Strategy links	Scottish Curriculum links	KS2 Levels
page 78	Shopping	To use a combination of operations to solve a money problem.	Working in pairs will encourage discussion about how this problem can be tackled using a variety of methods.	Problems involving 'real life', money or measures: Use all four operations to solve problems involving money. Place value, ordering and rounding: Multiply a positive integer by 100.	Problem-solving and enquiry – Level D	AT2 Level 4
page 79	Sharing the bill	To use a combination of operations to solve a money problem.	A calculator can be used for this activity but the children will need to read the display to two decimal places. As an extension, work out how much service charge is paid on each bill from Greens Fish Restaurant.	Problems involving 'real life', money or measures: Use all four operations to solve problems involving money.	Problem-solving and enquiry – Level E	AT2 Level 5
page 80	Cold days	To solve a problem using the available data.	Children need to be familiar with negative numbers related to temperature and a number line with negative numbers would be useful. Encourage the children to develop their own ideas on how to represent the information graphically.	Organising and using data: organise, represent and interpret data in tables, charts and graphs.	Information handling – Level B	AT4 Level 3
page 81	PE teams	To interpret data in a table.	Children need understand division and the concept of a remainder.	Organising and using data: Organise, represent and interpret data in tables, charts and graphs.	Information handling – Level B	AT4 Level 3
page 82	Flaming June	Create and interpret data in a chart.	This can be used as a whole-class activity by producing a large chart. The children can use the data from their weather chart to produce other graphs, such as bar charts. They could make predictions about how many sunny and/or wet days there will be in the month.	Organising and using data: Organise, represent and interpret data in tables, charts and graphs.	Information handling – Level B/C	AT4 Level 2/3
page 83	Favourite sports	To create and interpret data in a graph.	Children need to be able to tally accurately and the graphs can be produced using the computer.	Organising and using data: Organise, represent and interpret data in tables, charts and graphs.	Information handling – Level B/C	AT4 Level 2/3
page 84	Fixture list	To solve a problem by interpreting data.	Check that the children have managed to get all the permutations. The children may have to be reminded that the teams cannot play themselves. Answers: 6; 12; 8; 20; 42; 512.	Organising and using data: Solve a problem by organising, representing and interpreting data in tables, charts and graphs.	Information handling – Level C	AT4 Level 3/4
page 85	Tallying	To collect information quickly.	A useful follow-up exercise is for the children to devise their own data collection using tallying. Answers: 49; 171; 1.00 pm / 2.00 pm; 8.00 am / 9.00 am; 1.00 pm / 2.00 pm.	Organising and using data: Solve a problem by organising, representing and interpreting data in tables, charts and graphs.	Information handling – Level C	AT4 Level 3/4
page 86	Heads and tails	To solve a problem by collecting and interpreting data.	Encourage the children to predict how the results might changes as the number of tosses increases. Compare all the results. How many times did the coins land on 'heads' and how many times on 'tails'?	Organising and using data: Solve a problem by organising, representing and interpreting data in tables, charts and graphs.	Information handling – Level C	AT4 Level 3/4
page 87	Happy birthday	To solve a problem by collecting the appropriate data.	Children will use the mean average for this activity but they could discuss the mode and median averages following the activity.	Organising and using data: Solve a problem by organising, representing and interpreting data in tables, charts and graphs.	Information handling – Level C/D	AT4 Level 4
page 88	Watching television	To collect data and present it in a frequency graph.	Children will need to know how to construct a frequency graph. They could use graph paper or even an appropriate computer application. They should look for other notable points that emerge from their study and suggest possible reasons for these results.	Organising and using data: Solve a problem by organising, representing and interpreting data in tables, charts and graphs.	Information handling – Level C/D	AT4 Level 4
page 89	Mini sports	To solve a problem by interpreting data.	This activity gives practice in ordering decimal places. Some children will benefit from creating their own data from a class mini sports session.	Organising and using data: Solve a problem by organising, representing and interpreting data in tables, charts and graphs.	Information handling – Level C/D	AT4 Level 4
page 90	Pie charts	To collect data and present it on a pie chart.	A computer-generated pie chart program would be useful. Assistance with the division is given on the page as the charts are marked with the hours on the clock face.	Organising and using data: Solve a problem by organising, representing and interpreting data in tables, charts and graphs.	Information handling – Level C/D	AT4 Level 4

Page	Activity	Objective	Teachers' notes	National Numeracy Strategy links	Scottish Curriculum links	KS2 Levels
Page 91	New shoes	To solve a problem by extracting and using data.	Some additional work on range, median, mode and mean will be needed before this activity. Encourage the children to think why such data is collected; stock control, for example. This activity can also be applied to collecting classroom data. Answers: range = 5; median= 9½; mode = 9; mean = about 9½.	Handling data: Represent, extract and interpret data in a graph or chart.	Problem-solving and enquiry – Level D	AT4 Level 4
Page 92	Venn diagrams	To solve a problem by extracting and using data.	This is ideal for children working in pairs. Some revision of key terms may be needed. Answers: 25; 20, 28; 15, 6; 4, 16; 9; 36.	Handling data: Represent, extract and interpret data in a Venn diagram.	Problem-solving and enquiry – Level D	AT4 Level 4
Page 93	Curved graphs	To interpret data using graphs.	Remind children how to calculate area before they start this activity. The children may find it unusual to draw curved graphs as most graphs at primary level use straight lines. Answers: area of square (table) 1, 4, 9, 16, 25, 36; 6.25cm²; 12.25 cm²; 20.25 cm²; 2.23cm, 3.87cm, 4.47cm.	Handling data: Represent, extract and interpret data in a graph.	Problem-solving and enquiry – Level D/E	AT4 Level 5
Page 94	Production costs	To interpret data using graphs.	Work in pairs with adult support to explain the concepts involved – this is a difficult activity.	Handling data: Represent, extract and interpret data in a graph or chart.	Problem-solving and enquiry – Level E	AT4 Level 5
Page 95	Totals	To interpret from tables.	You might need to make a 7–12 die by sticking labelled masking tape onto a conventional die. Investigate all the possible ways for making each total.	Handling data: Represent, extract and interpret data in a graph or chart, and use the language associated with probability.	Problem-solving and enquiry – Level D/E	AT4 Level 5
Page 96	Fishy pictures	To explore shapes and patterns.	Children need to be familiar with the vocabulary of 2-D shapes. It is also important for them to understand that the shape names refer both to regular and irregular shapes.	Shape and space: Make and describe shapes and patterns.	Shape, position and movement – Level B/C	AT3 Level 2/3
Page 97	Shape tree	To classify 3-D shapes	Some children may need to physically sort the shapes. You could mix 2-D and 3-D shapes, and the children may wish to use their own criteria to sort the shapes.	Shape and space: Classify and describe 3-D shapes, referring to their properties.	Shape, position and movement – Level C	AT3 Level 3
Page 98	Boxes	To relate cubes and solid shapes.	You will need a collection of cardboard boxes. This activity explores the different types of net that could be used to make a box. Demonstrate how to open out a box by carefully undoing each of the glued sides. The children could investigate the nets and devise a net to make their own box.	Shape and space: Make and describe shapes and patterns.	Shape, position and movement – Level B/C	AT3 Level 2/3
Page 99	Structures with cubes	To begin to understand symmetry in structures.	It might be useful to try to draw the structures on squared paper. The children need to understand the term 'plane of symmetry'.	Shape and space: Identify and sketch lines of symmetry.	Shape, position and movement – Level B	AT3 Level 3
Page 100	Buried treasure	To find a position on a grid using compass points.	The children will need to know the points of the compass before this activity. It might be useful to use counters or small cards with the treasure names to place on the grid.	Shape and space: Recognise and use compass points and find the position on a grid.	Shape, position and movement – Level A/B	AT3 Level 3
Page 101	Chocolate pieces	To understand that there are different ways to divide a whole into fractions, and that each part does not need to be identical in shape.	It might be useful to encourage children to use squared paper to draw the whole shape and then colour the irregular line that cuts it in half. Practical experience of common fractions is necessary.	Shape and space: Make shapes and discuss their properties.	Shape, position and movement – Level C	AT3 Level 3/4
Page 102	Draw the other half	To begin to discuss the properties of lines of symmetry.	Use a mirror to help the children understand reflective symmetry.	Shape and space: Sketch the reflection of a simple shape in a mirror.	Shape, position and movement – Level C	AT3 Level 3/4
Page 103	Lines of symmetry	To begin to discuss the properties of lines of symmetry.	If you want to avoid excessive folding and would rather the children draw lines of symmetry you will have to make several copies of the page for folding, with an unfolded copy to record results.	Shape and space: Identify and sketch lines of symmetry.	Shape, position and movement – Level C	AT3 Level 3/4

SCHOLASTIC
www.scholastic.co.uk

Page	Activity	Objective	Teachers' notes	National Numeracy Strategy links	Scottish Curriculum links	KS2 Levels
page 104	Rotating a shape	To begin to understand the principles of rotation.	Check carefully that the children understand what they have to do.	Shape and space: Visualise 2-D drawings and where a shape will be after rotation.	Shape, position and movement – Level C	AT3 Level 3/4
page 105	Symmetry patterns	To recognise symmetry and complete symmetrical patterns.	These patterns can be created using lines or by colouring in squares or parts of squares. The children could also try different types of mathematical paper or folding the paper differently.	Shape and space: Complete symmetrical patterns with one or two lines of symmetry.	Shape, position and movement – Level C/D	AT3 Level 3/4
pages 105, 106 and 107	Symmetry dominoes – the game and Symmetry dominoes – 1 and 2	To recognise symmetry and complete symmetrical patterns.	The cards should be produced on thin card and the game needs to be played on a large table. The children could develop the set by adding their own symmetry domino cards.	Shape and space: Complete symmetrical patterns with one or two lines of symmetry.	Shape, position and movement – Level C/D	AT3 Level 3/4
page 108	Spiral loops	To recognise position and directions.	Children could devise their own number patterns and investigate what happens when they are used for the lengths in this activity.	Shape and space: Complete symmetrical patterns with two lines of symmetry.	Shape, position and movement – Level C/D	AT3 Level 3/4
page 109	Mystery picture	To read and plot coordinates.	Remind the children to read the x coordinate before the y coordinate.	Shape and space: Read and plot coordinates in the first quadrant.	Shape, position and movement – Level D/E	AT3 Level 4/5
page 110	Plotting shapes	To interpret data using graphs.	The children could be given a second sheet to plot their own shapes, and then to try doubling them.	Shape and space: Read and plot coordinates in the first quadrant.	Shape, position and movement – Level D/E	AT3 Level 5
page 111	Cubes and cuboids	To devise and visualise properties of solid shapes.	It might be useful to have interlocking cubes available. The children need to be familiar with handling cubes to find volume. Ask each child to make three of four cubes and cuboids. Write the dimensions for each on a piece of card and play a matching game.	Shape and space: Describe properties of solid shapes.	Shape, position and movement – Level D/E	AT3 Level 5
page 112	Rotating shapes	To devise and visualise properties of solid shapes.	It might be useful to have interlocking cubes available. Use rotation and reflection as ways of fitting on the shapes.	Shape and space: Recognise where a shape will be after reflection, rotation and translation.	Shape, position and movement – Level D/E	AT3 Level 4/5
page 113	Guess the weight	To read scales and use measures of standard units.	It would be useful for the children to know what set weights, such as 10g, 50g and 100g, feel like so that they can estimate more accurately. Children should be familiar with reading scales that include grams. The children should be encouraged to estimate before they weigh the item.	Measures: Record estimates and use grams as a unit of measurement.	Number, money and measurement – Level B	AT3 Level 3
page 114	What could you use?	To use different instruments to measure length accurately.	Children should be encouraged to compare results and ask questions if they are measuring the same thing but get a different length. Ensure that appropriate measuring devices are available, including flexible and inflexible tools, and a trundle wheel. Show the children how to use the devices if they are unsure.	Measures: Suggest suitable units and measuring equipment.	Number, money and measurement – Level B	
page 115	Gifts	To compare standard units of mass.	The children will need to be familiar with adding two-digit and one-digit numbers together. Have a few real packages for the children to investigate first.	Measures: Use, read and write standard metric units. Making decisions: Choose and use appropriate number operations to solve problems.	Number, money and measurement – Level B	AT3 Level 3

Page	Activity	Objective	Teachers' notes	National Numeracy Strategy links	Scottish Curriculum links	KS2 Levels
pages 116 and 117	Reading a scale 1 and 2	To continue to understand how to read different scales.	Discuss what each mark or space on a scale might mean on each device, for example a scale on a weighing scale or a measuring cylinder.	Measures: Record estimates and readings from scales to a degree of accuracy.	Number, money and measurement – Level C	AT3 Level 3/4
page 118	Telling the time	To read the time from an analogue clock.	It may be necessary to explain how to tell the time in 5-minute intervals on an analogue clock.	Measures: Read the time to 5 minutes on an analogue clock.	Number, money and measurement – Level C	AT3 Level 3/4
page 119	On time	To estimate and check times.	This activity uses both digital and analogue times. Answers: 9.20; 4.25; 1 hour 5 minutes; 6.30.	Measures: Read the time on analogue and digital clocks.	Number, money and measurement – Level C	AT3 Level 3/4
page 120	Plasticine weights	To record mass by using appropriate weights.	It will be helpful if children made more than one of some of the weights.	Measures: Suggest suitable units and measuring equipment to measure mass.	Number, money and measurement – Level C/D	AT3 Level 3/4
page 121	How much time?	To measure time accurately.	Working in pairs would help make the timings more accurate. Make sure children predict the time first. Did they find it easier to estimate the time when doing or watching the activity?	Measures: Estimate and check times using seconds and minutes.	Number, money and measurement – Level C/D	AT3 Level 3/4
page 122	Tickets	To use 24-hour clock notation.	The children need to be familiar with 24-hour time. Make a collection of real tickets and ask the children to explain the times on them. They could make up their own ticket and explain the times on it to a friend.	Measures: Use 24-hour clock notation.	Number, money and measurement – Level C/D	AT3 Level 4
page 123	Litres and millilitres	To measure to the nearest millilitre.	Children must be able to convert from millilitres to litres and back again. Answers: (litre labels) 0.5l, 0.2l, 2.25l, 1.2l, 1l, 1.5l, 0.25l; (millimetre labels) 250ml, 500ml, 500ml, 1000ml, 100ml, 2500ml, 200ml.	Measures: Know and use the relationships between familiar units of capacity, and convert smaller units to larger units.	Number, money and measurement – Level C/D	AT3 Level 4
page 124	Volume problems (cards)	To work with metric units for capacity and volume.	A calculator would be useful for this activity. The six cards can be cut out and laminated for individual or group work. The children could make up volume problem cards of their own for others to solve.	Measures: Use, read and write standard metric units and the relationships between them. Making decisions: Choose and use appropriate number operations and appropriate ways of calculating to solve problems.	Number, money and measurement – Level D/E	AT3 Level 4/5
page 125	Matching	To appreciate different times and how they are recorded.	A selection of different analogue and digital watches and clock faces are useful for this activity. The children should be familiar with telling time on both analogue and digital clocks to 5-minute intervals.	Measures: Read the time on an analogue clock and use 24-hour clock notation.	Number, money and measurement – Level D/E	AT3 Level 4/5
page 126	Find the perimeter	To calculate the perimeter of various shapes.	Children must understand that they have to use a common unit of measure to do these calculations and may have to convert some of the side lengths. They will need to know how to convert between metres, centimetres and kilometres. Answers: A 3486m; B 2900m; C 20000m; D 157.9km; E 642m; F 3334m.	Measures: Calculate the perimeter of shapes; convert smaller units to larger units, and larger units to smaller units.	Number, money and measurement – Level E	AT3 Level 5
page 127	Circles	To calculate the circumference of various circles.	Do some practice circles to check for accuracy. The children should realise that the diameter will fit 'three and a bit' times around the circumference of a circle. If you divide the circumference (c) of any circle by its diameter (d), the result is 3.14 (to two decimal places). This number is known as pi and its symbol is Π. Therefore c = Πd. Answers: A, r = 2cm, d = 4cm, c = 12.56cm; B, r = 3cm, d = 6cm, c = 18.84cm; C, r = 4cm, d = 8cm, c = 25.12cm; D, r = 5cm, d = 10cm, c = 31.40cm.	Measures: Use, read and write standard metric units. Reasoning and generalising about numbers or shapes: Solve mathematical problems or puzzles, recognise and explain patterns and relationships, generalise and predict.	Number, money and measurement – Level E	AT3 Level 5

SCHOLASTIC
www.scholastic.co.uk

Name _____

Looking for patterns

❖ Look carefully at the number sequences below. Write in the next 3 numbers for each.

❖ Write a sentence for each pattern to explain what is happening.

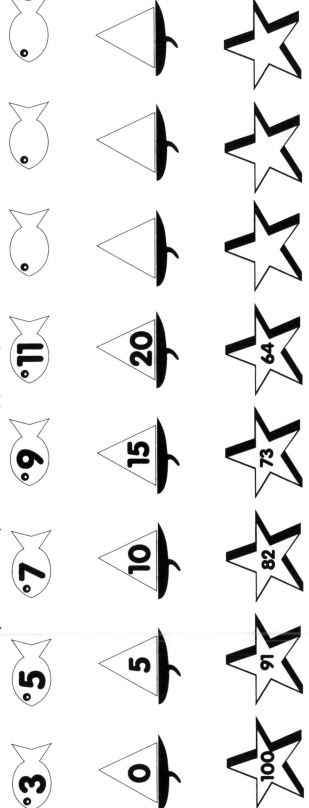

❖ Make up some number sequences for other children to try.

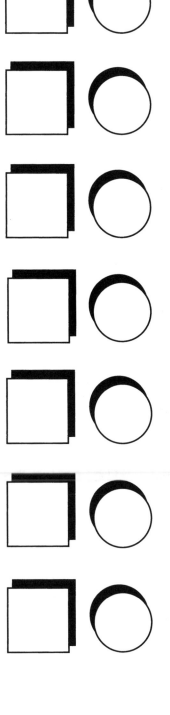

SCHOLASTIC
www.scholastic.co.uk

Name _____

Mr Mystery Maker

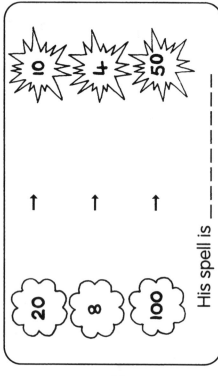

❋ What spell has he cast on these numbers?

20   8   100

↑   ↑   ↑

10   4   50

His spell is _____

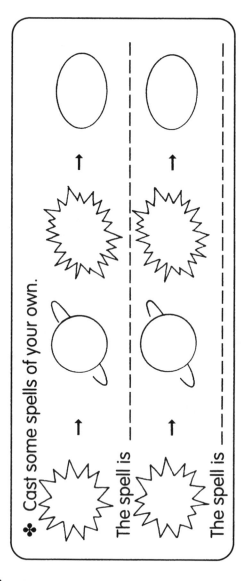

❋ Cast some spells of your own.

The spell is _____

The spell is _____

Mr Mystery Maker, the magician, has cast a spell on some numbers. Can you find out what he has done to them?

2 has turned into 6

5 has turned into 15

7 has turned into 21

His spell is _____

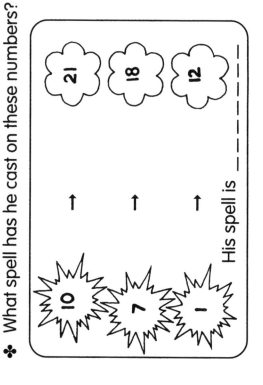

♣ What spell has he cast on these numbers?

21   18   12

↑   ↑   ↑

10   7   1

His spell is _____

NO FUSS PHOTOCOPIABLE

SCHOLASTIC
www.scholastic.co.uk

Name _____

Tile designs

◆ Use green, yellow and blue to colour in the shape below.

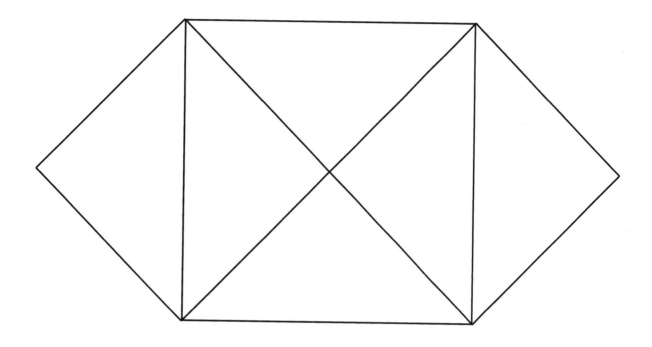

◆ What fraction of your pattern is coloured in:

• green? _____

• yellow? _____

• blue? _____

◆ This time colour in the shape below so that:

• $\frac{1}{2}$ is blue;

• $\frac{1}{4}$ is red;

• $\frac{1}{8}$ is green;

• $\frac{1}{8}$ is yellow.

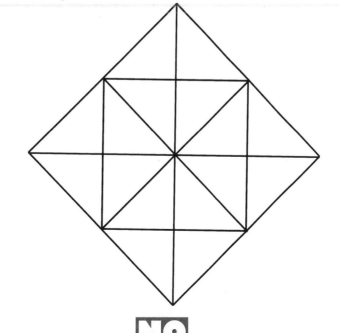

SCHOLASTIC
www.scholastic.co.uk

NO FUSS
PHOTOCOPIABLE

Name _____

Fraction flags – I

You will need: a copy of the 'Fraction flags – 2' sheet and some colouring pencils.

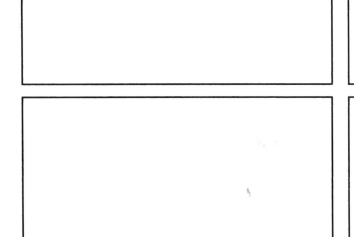

◆ Colour each flag card on the 'Fraction flags – 2' sheet in a different colour. Then cut each card into the pieces shown.

◆ Cover your 'whole' flag card with pieces from two different coloured cards. Find four different ways of doing this and record them on the flags below.

◆ Now cover the 'whole' flag card with pieces from three different coloured cards. Find four different ways of doing this and record them below.

SCHOLASTIC
www.scholastic.co.uk

Name _____

Fraction flags – 2

The 'whole' flag

NO FUSS PHOTOCOPIABLE

Bigger and **bigger**

♣ Multiply the numbers given below by 10 and by 100.
Fill in the table:

Number	Number multiplied by 10	Number multiplied by 100	Can you predict multiplied by 1000?
3			
8			
20			
32			

♣ Fill in the numbers that have been
multiplied by 10 and 100:

Number	Number multiplied by 10	Number multiplied by 100
	20	200
	430	4300
	670	6700
	4800	48000

♣ Fill in the missing numbers:

Number	Number multiplied by 10	Number multiplied by 100
17		1700
	420	4200
	620	
30	300	
	540	

♣ You could make a missing number table for your friend to fill in.

NO FUSS PHOTOCOPIABLE

■ SCHOLASTIC
www.scholastic.co.uk

New uniforms

The king has ordered new uniforms for his guards.

The first guard's tunic must be $\frac{1}{2}$ red and $\frac{1}{2}$ blue.

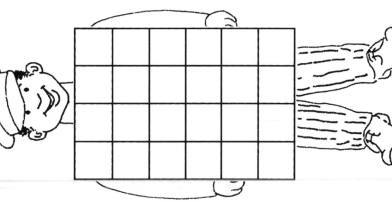

The second guard's tunic must be $\frac{1}{3}$ red, $\frac{1}{3}$ blue and $\frac{1}{3}$ green.

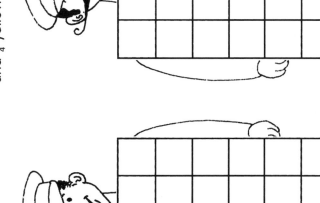

The third guard's tunic must be $\frac{1}{4}$ red, $\frac{1}{4}$ blue, $\frac{1}{4}$ green and $\frac{1}{4}$ yellow.

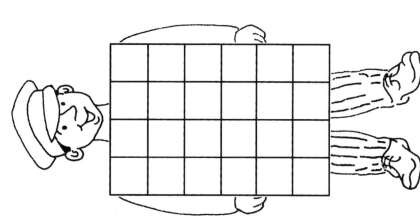

The fourth guard's tunic must be $\frac{1}{8}$ red, $\frac{1}{8}$ blue, $\frac{1}{8}$ green, $\frac{1}{8}$ yellow, $\frac{1}{8}$ brown, $\frac{1}{8}$ black, $\frac{1}{8}$ orange and $\frac{1}{8}$ purple.

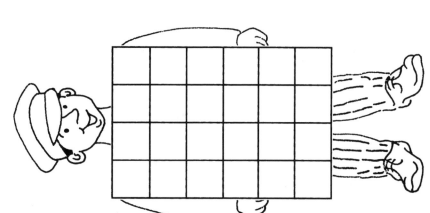

♣ Could you make a different set of tunics for the guards to wear in processions?

SCHOLASTIC
www.scholastic.co.uk

NO FUSS
PHOTOCOPIABLE

Name _____

Slices of pie

A game for two players.

Each of you will need: the pie dish and 'Slices of pie' playing pieces below cut out, and one spinner between you, copied on to card.

I   Each put your set of cut out playing pieces on to your pie dish.

2   In turn, spin the spinner and take off from your dish the slice, or slices, of pie that equal the fraction shown on the spinner. If you cannot take off the correct fraction of pie, miss a go.

3   The winner is the first one to clear their plate.

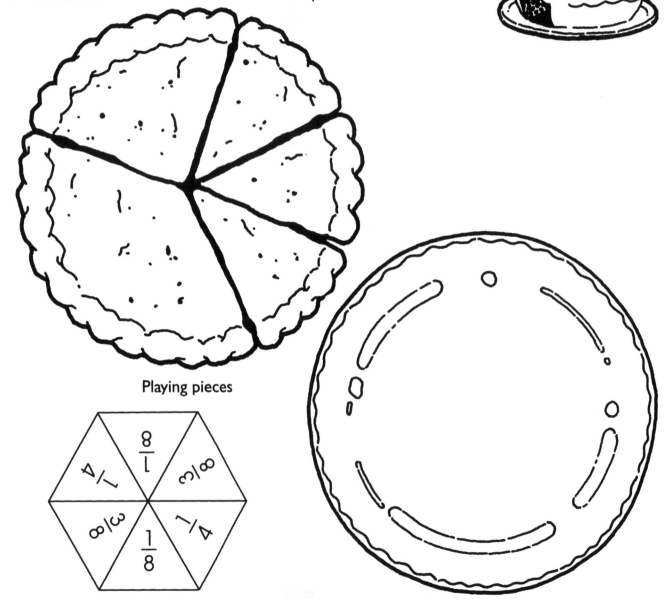

Playing pieces

Pie dish

SCHOLASTIC
www.scholastic.co.uk

Corner numbers

The numbers on the corners of these shapes must:
- total the centre number;
- be equal.

◆ Find out what the missing numbers must be and fill them in.

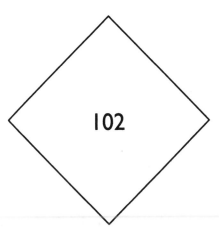

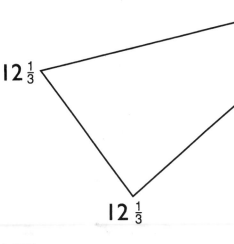

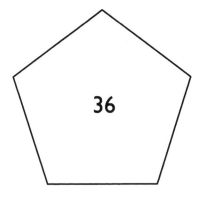

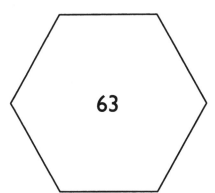

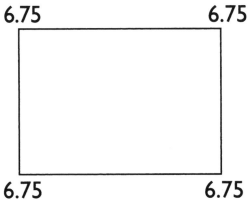

◆ Make up some more puzzles like these for someone else to try.

Name _____

Function mazes

Here is a function maze.

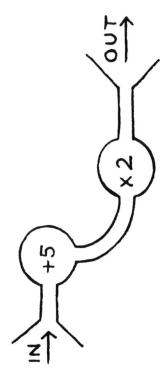

Feed in 2 and 14 comes out.

♣ What happens when these numbers go into this maze?

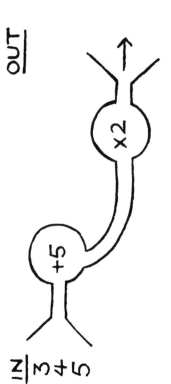

♣ Now try this maze.

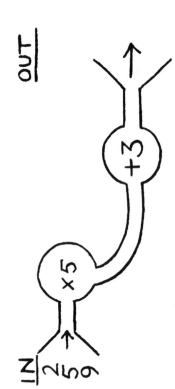

This maze has three functions.
♣ Try feeding in these numbers:

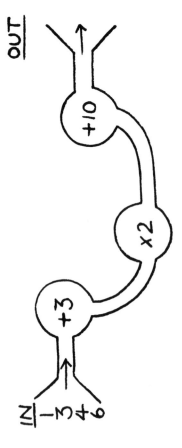

Make up some function mazes of your own and try them on a friend.

NO FUSS PHOTOCOPIABLE

■SCHOLASTIC
www.scholastic.co.uk

Just two

3.1 1.8 + 1.3	4.6	2.1	4.0
1.8	2.3	3.7	1.6
1.1	2.5	4.3	3.0
5.2	3.6	2.4	1.9

◆ To make **one** of the numbers on the grid above, choose **two** numbers from the bag below.

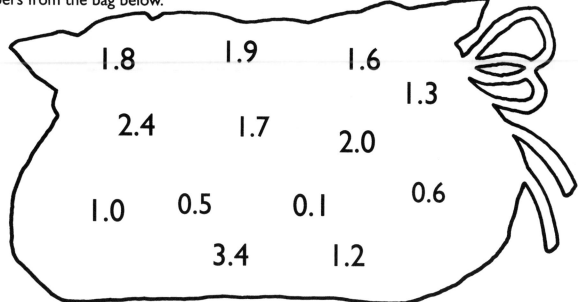

1.8   1.9   1.6   1.3

2.4   1.7   2.0

1.0   0.5   0.1   0.6

3.4   1.2

◆ Record the two numbers that you added to make each of the numbers on the grid. You may use a number as often as you like. One has been done for you.

SCHOLASTIC
www.scholastic.co.uk

NO FUSS
PHOTOCOPIABLE

Name _____

Box the digits

◆ Place the digits 1, 2, 3 and 4 in the boxes to make the number sentences correct. Use each digit once in each sentence.

☐ . ☐ + ☐ . ☐ = 5 . 5

☐ . ☐ + ☐ . ☐ = 6 . 4

◆ In the next two number sentences use 1, 2, 3, 4, but one of these digits is used twice in each sentence.

☐ . ☐ + ☐ . ☐ = ☐ . 7

☐ . ☐ + ☐ . ☐ = 7 . ☐

◆ Use the digits 1, 2, 3, 4 and 5 to complete the next two number sentences. Again, some digits can be used twice.

☐ . ☐ + ☐ . ☐ ☐ = 6 . 54

☐ . ☐ − ☐ . ☐ ☐ = ☐ . 8 ☐

◆ Place the digits in the boxes to show fractions and their decimal equivalents; like this:

• Use 1, 2, 4, 5

$$\frac{1}{4} = 0 . \boxed{2}\,\boxed{5}$$

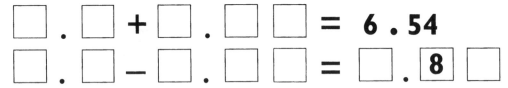

• Use 3, 4, 5, 7

$$\frac{\square}{\square} = 0 . \square\,\square$$

• Use 2, 3, 5, 7

$$\frac{\square}{\square} = \square . \square$$

• Use 5, 6, 7, 8

$$\frac{\square}{\square} = 0 . \square\,\square$$

• Use 1, 2, 3, 5

$$\frac{\square}{\square} = \square . \square$$

• Use 1, 5, 8, 9

$$\frac{\square}{\square} = \square . \square$$

• Use 1, 5, 6, 9

$$\frac{\square}{\square} = \square . \square$$

• Use 2, 4, 5, 9

$$\frac{\square}{\square} = \square . \square$$

• Use 1, 4, 5, 6

$$\frac{\square}{\square} = \square . \square$$

• Use 1, 2, 5, 8, 9

$$\frac{\square}{\square} = 1 . \square\,\square\,\square$$

NO FUSS PHOTOCOPIABLE

SCHOLASTIC
www.scholastic.co.uk

Bingo

A game for two to six players.

You will need: some counters, the digit cards below, the 'Bingo cards' page cut into individual cards and a pencil and paper for each player for working out.

I Shuffle the bingo cards and deal a bingo card to each player.

2 Shuffle the digit cards and place them face down in a pile.

3 Turn over the top digit card. Each player has ten minutes to make the numbers on their bingo card using just the three digits on the card. Place a counter on any total made.

For example:

$$\boxed{7\ 2\ 3} \rightarrow \quad 72 \div 3 = 24$$
$$7 + 2 - 3 = 6$$

4 Scoring:
- I point for each number made;
- 2 bonus points for two numbers side by side;
- 5 bonus points for a line of three numbers.

5 Play four rounds. The winner is the person with most points at the end of round four.

Digit cards

7 2 3	**2 8 9**
1 6 4	**9 7 1**
5 4 6	**3 5 8**

Name _____

Bingo cards

1	4	8
9	15	16
21	■	25

1	2	6
8	10	■
12	19	26

3	4	6
7	15	■
17	23	29

3	7	8
■	12	14
24	25	34

2	■	10
12	14	15
19	24	37

3	4	10
16	23	■
25	39	13

SCHOLASTIC
www.scholastic.co.uk

Name _____

Four ways

Each box below has a rule at the top.

◆ Using this rule, record four more ways in each box that you can make the target number in the centre. Some examples have been done for you.

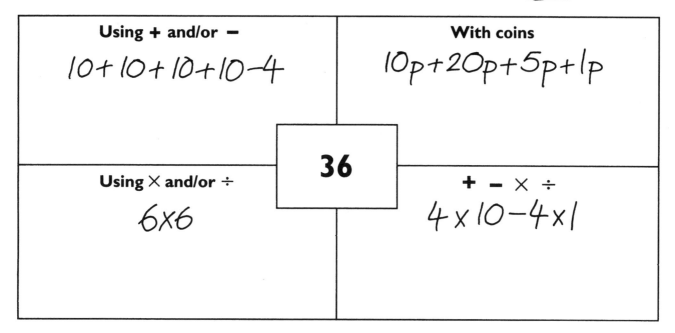

Using + and/or −	With coins
10+10+10+10−4	10p+20p+5p+1p

36

Using × and/or ÷	+ − × ÷
6×6	4×10−4×1

◆ Now try to make this target number.

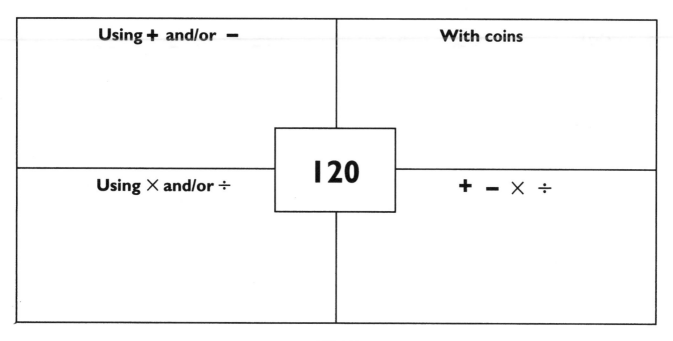

Using + and/or −	With coins

120

Using × and/or ÷	+ − × ÷

■SCHOLASTIC
www.scholastic.co.uk

NO FUSS
PHOTOCOPIABLE

| 0 . 14 |
| 0 . 35 |
| 0 . 07 |
| 1 . 03 |
| 1 . 13 |
| 0 . 71 |
| 0 . 24 |
| 0 . 98 |

DECIMAL NUMBERS

♣ Cut out the number cards on the right hand side of this page. Deal them into two piles.

0.14

♣ Look at the numbers in each set and estimate which has the highest total. Now check your guess. A calculator may be useful.

♣ Can you make the two piles have equal totals? Can you make them nearly equal?

♣ Shuffle the two sets together and order the cards from highest to lowest.

♣ Make another 4 cards to be included in this pack. The numbers you choose to put on them must be within the range of your highest to lowest cards. Then answer the same questions again.

NO FUSS PHOTOCOPIABLE

SCHOLASTIC
www.scholastic.co.uk

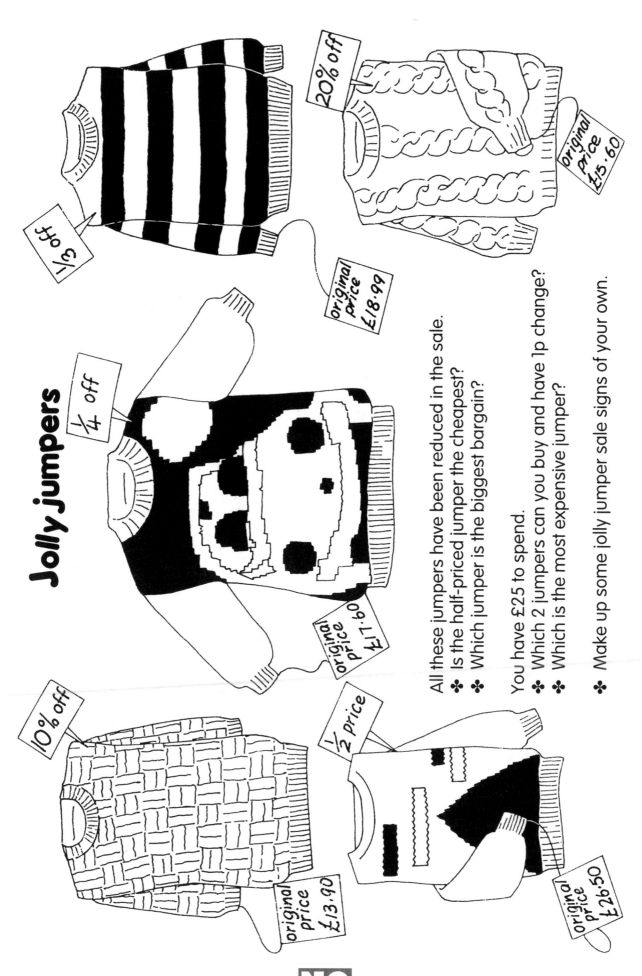

Jolly jumpers

20% off

original price £5.60

1/3 off

original price £18.99

1/4 off

original price £17.60

10% off

original price £13.90

1/2 price

original price £26.50

All these jumpers have been reduced in the sale.

❖ Is the half-priced jumper the cheapest?
❖ Which jumper is the biggest bargain?

You have £25 to spend.

❖ Which 2 jumpers can you buy and have 1p change?
❖ Which is the most expensive jumper?

❖ Make up some jolly jumper sale signs of your own.

Decimal fun!

2.3	0.17
5.4	1.05
1.5	7.5
1.2	4.2
0.6	2.1
0.8	6.9
3.9	5.3

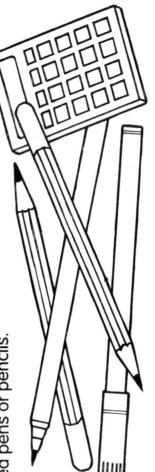

✱ For this decimal game you will need: a partner, a calculator and two different coloured pens or pencils.

♣ Player A chooses two numbers from the panel on the right and decides to either multiply or divide one by the other. For example 2.3 × 1.2 = 2.76. This is then marked on the number line.

♣ Player B then chooses two numbers and again either multiplies or divides one by the other and marks the answer on the line.

♣ The first player to get three marks in a row, without any of their opponents marks in between, wins.

(If the answer is off the range 1–10, then that player misses a go.)

NO FUSS PHOTOCOPIABLE

■**SCHOLASTIC**
www.scholastic.co.uk

Which would you rather have?

◆ Put a ring around the amount below that gives you the larger total of each pair.

- $\frac{1}{2}$ of 17   a quarter of 35

- 25% of 120   a third of 93

- a tenth of 36 $\frac{1}{5}$ of 19

- $\frac{2}{3}$ of 63   two fifths of 100

- 0.5 of 72 $\frac{3}{4}$ of 52

- 40% of 200   0.75 of 80

- $\frac{4}{5}$ of 1   0.2 of 3

Grand total of all the larger ones _____

◆ Target 300

•   Now choose any of the above to make a grand total that is to be as near to 300 as possible.

•   Ring all your choices in a different colour.

> Use this space to do any working out.

> Show here how you worked this out.

My closest grand total is _____

Making a tables game

✣ Roll two (1 – 6) dice and multiply your scores together.
✣✣ Put the answer into one of the spaces on the grid below.
✣✣✣ Keep rolling the dice. Each time you get a different answer fill it in on the grid.
✣✣ Now think of a way of using this grid for a tables game. Write the rules on a piece of paper. Test it on some friends.

NO FUSS PHOTOCOPIABLE

SCHOLASTIC
www.scholastic.co.uk

Name _____

Best guess

Here are some sums and some estimates of the answers.

❖ For each sum, decide which you think is the best estimate of the answer, then use a calculator to check.

❖ Write down the true answer. Was yours a good or bad guess?

Sum	Estimates				True answer	Good or bad guess
53 + 28	60	70	80	90		
61 + 32	80	90	100	110		
96 − 31	50	60	70	80		
49 + 22	60	70	80	90		
95 − 48	40	50	60	70		
73 + 58	110	120	130	140		
36 + 16	40	50	60	70		
71 − 49	20	30	40	50		
67 + 58	100	110	120	130		

❖ Now work with a friend.

❖ Think of a sum and write it down.

❖ Let your friend make an estimate of the answer. Then check the answer with a calculator.

❖ Take it in turns to make up sums for each other. Decide how close a guess must be to the true answer to see who wins each round.

❖ Record your game like this:

Sum	Estimate	True answer	Good or bad guess

If your want to, continue on the back of this sheet.

Name _____

Number chains

| 3 | 4 | 7 | 11 | 18 |

You get each number in the boxes above by adding up the previous two numbers. For example: $3 + 4 = 7$, $4 + 7 = 11$, $7 + 11 = 18$.

✤ Complete these boxes using the same rule.

✤ Make up some number chains of your own.

SCHOLASTIC
www.scholastic.co.uk

Crafty corners

Name _____

* Look at the top square and rectangle which have been drawn on the table square.

* Multiply the numbers in the opposite corners.

  • Square: $2 \times 6 =$

    $3 \times 4 =$

  • Rectangle: $6 \times 18 =$

    $9 \times 12 =$

* What do you notice?

* Check your results for the other square and rectangle.

* Try the same thing with squares and rectangles of your own.

1	2	3	4	5	6	7	8	9	10
2	4	6	8	10	12	14	16	18	20
3	6	9	12	15	18	21	24	27	30
4	8	12	16	20	24	28	32	36	40
5	10	15	20	25	30	35	40	45	50
6	12	18	24	30	36	42	48	54	60
7	14	21	28	35	42	49	56	63	70
8	16	24	32	40	48	56	64	72	80
9	18	27	36	45	54	63	72	81	90
10	20	30	40	50	60	70	80	90	100

■SCHOLASTIC
www.scholastic.co.uk

NO FUSS
PHOTOCOPIABLE

Name _____

Which number?

There are three different ways to make 4 by multiplying two whole numbers together. They are 1 x 4, 2 x 2 and 4 x 1.

✲ Which number on the hundred board can you make in the most ways by multiplying two whole numbers?

1	2	3	4	5	6	7	8	9	10
11	12	13	14	15	16	17	18	19	20
21	22	23	24	25	26	27	28	29	30
31	32	33	34	35	36	37	38	39	40
41	42	43	44	45	46	47	48	49	50
51	52	53	54	55	56	57	58	59	60
61	62	63	64	65	66	67	68	69	70
71	72	73	74	75	76	77	78	79	80
81	82	83	84	85	86	87	88	89	90
91	92	93	94	95	96	97	98	99	100

NO FUSS

PHOTOCOPIABLE

■SCHOLASTIC
www.scholastic.co.uk

Name _____

Possible products

❖ Using two (1-6) dice, find all the possible products.

❖ How can you classify your results to ensure that all possible products have been considered?

❖ Now try using two (1-8) or (1-10) dice. How will the work you have already done with the (1-6) dice help you?

❖ Use the space below to design a pair of six-sided dice that will give products which include all the numbers from 1 to 17.

■ SCHOLASTIC
www.scholastic.co.uk

NO FUSS
PHOTOCOPIABLE

Matching the pairs

♣ Work out the answers to the sums below. Draw lines to join the sums that give the same answer.

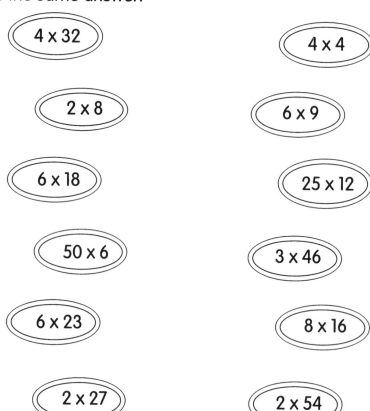

4 x 32

4 x 4

2 x 8

6 x 9

6 x 18

25 x 12

50 x 6

3 x 46

6 x 23

8 x 16

2 x 27

2 x 54

♣ Make up 2 pairs for yourself.

♣ Now look at this: 15 x 8 = 30 x 4 = 60 x 2 = 120 x 1

♣ Can you explore the following products in the same way, so that they end with something multiplied by 1?
14 x 8
17 x 6

NO FUSS
PHOTOCOPIABLE

SCHOLASTIC.
www.scholastic.co.uk

Name _____

In between

◆ Put the number in each box which is **half way between** the following numbers:

20		30
44		54
75		99
6		7
35		40
15cm		18cm
£1.20		£1.30

◆ The boxes now lie a **quarter of the way back from the highest number.** What numbers go in the boxes now?

0		20
65		85
8		9

◆ Put the number in each box which is **three tenths of the way from the lower number.**

30			40
58			78
6			7

Name _____

A shopkeeper has to check the stock in his shop every week. Can you help?
❖ Look at last week's stock list which is shown below.

❖ Now look at how many of each item were sold this week.
❖ Work out how many of each item there are left in stock. One has been done for you.

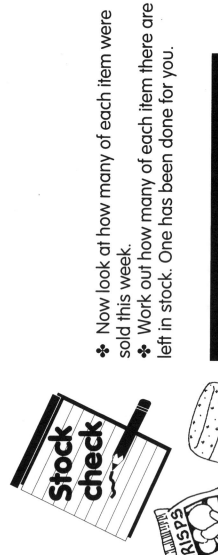

SALES (THIS WEEK)		
Item	**Sold**	**In stock**
biscuits	34 packets	38
coffee	15 jars	
crisps	298 bags	
sugar	100 packets	
choc ices	39 ices	
dog food	72 tins	
cat food	98 tins	
beans	200 tins	
soup	100 packets	
peas	48 bags	

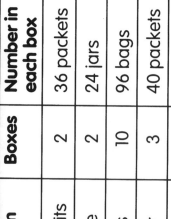
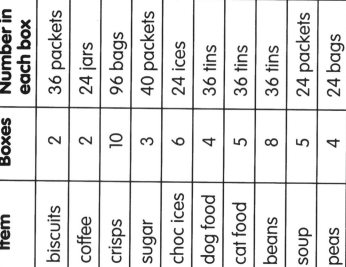

STOCK LIST (AT END OF LAST WEEK)		
Item	**Boxes**	**Number in each box**
biscuits	2	36 packets
coffee	2	24 jars
crisps	10	96 bags
sugar	3	40 packets
choc ices	6	24 ices
dog food	4	36 tins
cat food	5	36 tins
beans	8	36 tins
soup	5	24 packets
peas	4	24 bags

NO FUSS PHOTOCOPIABLE

SCHOLASTIC
www.scholastic.co.uk

Name _____

Can you calculate?

♣ Three answers are given below for each sum.
♣ Guess which is the correct answer, then check.
♣ Put a ring around the correct answer.

572 + 776 = ?   (1348)   (13480)   (1248)

1763 + 359 = ?   (21222)   (2122)   (4122)

5753 + 7742 = ?   (16495)   (13495)   (133495)

1156 - 94 = ?   (962)   (1162)   (1062)

3784 - 1402 = ?   (2382)   (2342)   (2682)

8794 - 363 = ?   (9157)   (5164)   (8431)

♣ Below you are given some answers. For each one, put a ring round the sum which you think gives that answer.

(8876)   643 + 8233 or 9639 - 1233 or 2423 + 7453

(2546)   5546 - 2546 or 6624 - 4078 or 1252 + 1394

(5003)   1500 + 503 or 233 + 4770 or 2261 + 2942

Name _____

Twenty

A game for two to four players.

You will need: a playing board (drawn as shown opposite) for each player and four sets of the 0–9 cards below, shuffled into one pack.

1 In turn, each player takes a card from the pack and places it on their playing board until all six spaces are filled. Once a card has been placed, it cannot be moved. The aim of the game is for the three numbers that you make on your playing board to total as near to 20 as possible.

2 The numbers are then added up and the totals compared. The player with the total nearest to 20 wins one point.

For example:

9	•	4
3	•	1
9	•	2
21	•	7

3 Every player **now** has five minutes to move their number cards around on the playing board to try and obtain another total closer to 20. The totals are compared again and the player with the total nearest to 20 wins one point.

You will need **four** sets of these digit cards.

0	1	2	3	4
5	6	7	8	9

NO FUSS PHOTOCOPIABLE

SCHOLASTIC
www.scholastic.co.uk

Name _____

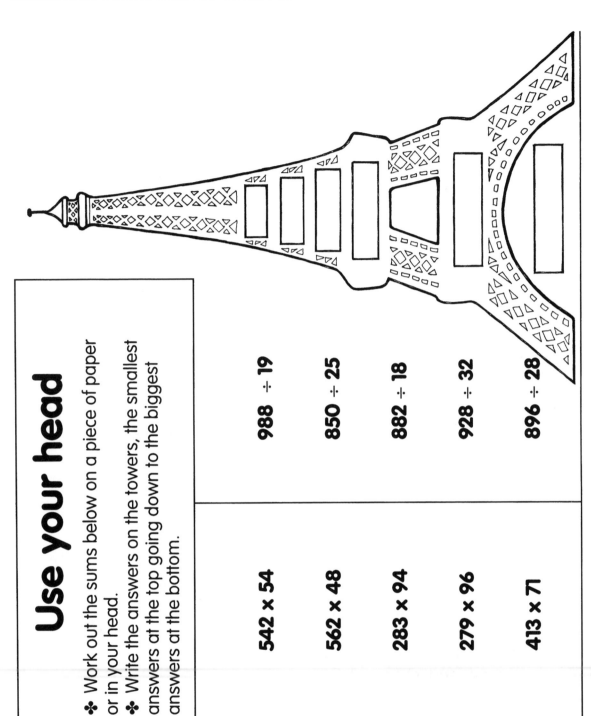

Use your head

♣ Work out the sums below on a piece of paper or in your head.
♣ Write the answers on the towers, the smallest answers at the top going down to the biggest answers at the bottom.

988 ÷ 19	542 × 54
850 ÷ 25	562 × 48
882 ÷ 18	283 × 94
928 ÷ 32	279 × 96
896 ÷ 28	413 × 71

♣ Make up some tower sums for a friend to try.

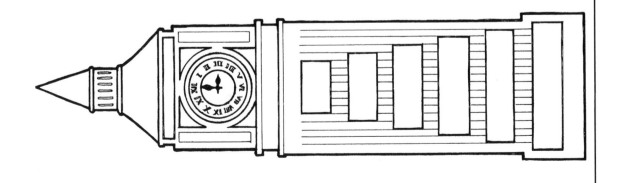

SCHOLASTIC
www.scholastic.co.uk

NO FUSS
PHOTOCOPIABLE

Name _____

Make it BIG

♣ Cut out the numbers on the right.
♣ Arrange the numbers 1, 2, 3, 4 and 5 in any order to give the greatest possible product.

For example:

☐ ☐ ☐   ☐ ☐ ☐ ☐
　☐ ☐　 or 　　　 ☐

_____　　_____
_____　　_____

♣ What is the smallest product possible?

♣ Use the digits 2, 3, 4, 5 and 6.
What is the largest product possible?
What is the smallest product possible?

♣ Use the digits 3, 4, 5, 6 and 7.
What is the largest product possible?
What is the smallest product possible?

♣ Is there a rule ? If so, can you explain it?

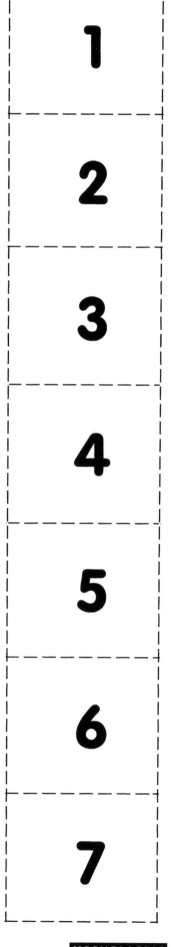

1

2

3

4

5

6

7

SCHOLASTIC
www.scholastic.co.uk

Name _____

Square numbers

❖ Complete this square number pattern up to 10 × 10.

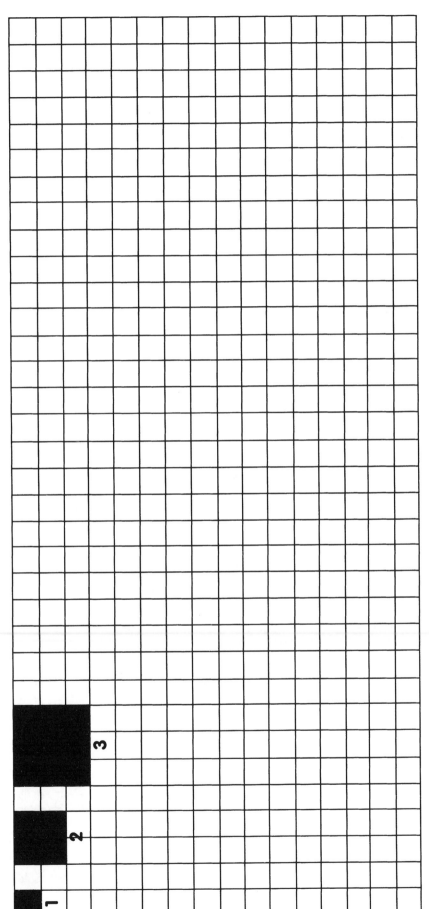

❖ Write out the sequence of square numbers and explore the pattern of differences between the numbers.

❖ ❖ Can you see a relationship? If so, explain what it is. Say how it develops and why.

📖 **SCHOLASTIC**
www.scholastic.co.uk

Square-eyed

225	121	169	900
784	49	441	81
289	1600	256	64
100	324	576	625

Circles:
11^2 9^2 8^2 24^2 17^2 15^2 25^2 16^2 40^2 28^2 13^2 7^2 30^2 18^2 21^2 10^2

You will need: about 20 counters.

♣ The aim of this game is to cover with counters four numbers on the grid in a line, vertically, horizontally or diagonally.

♣ To cover a number, find the number from the circles which equals it. For example, for 169 on the grid you would choose 13^2.

♣ Record the number you select and the number you are aiming to cover up.

♣ You may have only one attempt at matching a circle with a grid square each turn. The first person to cover four connecting numbers is the winner.

♣ With your partner, check all the pairs of numbers you have used.

NO FUSS
PHOTOCOPIABLE

SCHOLASTIC
www.scholastic.co.uk

Name _____

Which key?

You will need: a calculator.
In the number sentence below, the function keys are blank.

9 ☐ 3 ☐ 5 = 32

✤ Which two keys have to be pressed to give the right answer?

Here is the solution:

9 ☒ 3 ⊞ 5 = 32

✤ In each of these number sentences, insert the function keys needed
(+, −, ×, ÷) and then check your answers on the calculator.

1	5	☐	3	☐	4	= 32
2	6	☐	5	☐	7	= 7
3	8	☐	2	☐	2	= 5
4	10	☐	4	☐	8	= 14
5	5	☐	4	☐	2	= 10
6	20	☐	13	☐	3	= 21
7	30	☐	6	☐	19	= 24
8	56	☐	7	☐	4	= 4
9	9	☐	7	☐	20	= 43
10	70	☐	18	☐	2	= 26
11	96	☐	12	☐	8	= 64
12	100	☐	25	☐	3	= 25

Rolling dice

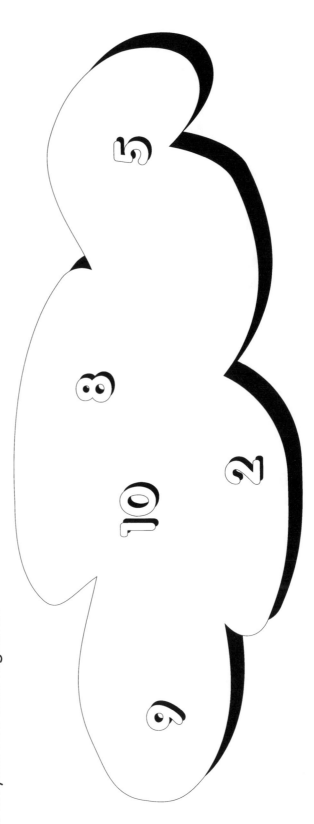

✤ Roll two (1 – 6) dice and add your scores together. What did you get?

✤ Is it possible to make all of the numbers from 0 – 12 in this way? Investigate and find out.

✤ Choose any one of the numbers below and find all the possible ways of making it by adding the scores on your two dice together.

5   8   10   2   6

✤ Can you find a way of checking that you have got all of the possible solutions?

NO FUSS PHOTOCOPIABLE

SCHOLASTIC
www.scholastic.co.uk

Dartboards

You have three darts to throw at this dartboard. Darts landing in the shaded ring count double.

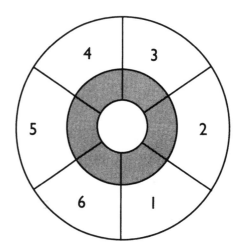

◆ What is the highest score you can get if each dart lands on the **same** number?

_____

◆ What is the highest score you can get if you hit a **different** number with each dart?

_____

◆ Write down as many ways as you can of scoring 26 with three darts.

◆ If all three darts hit the board each time, which numbers below the highest score **cannot** be made?

◆ Arrange numbers on this board so that all the scores are between 20 and 90, with three darts hitting the board each time.

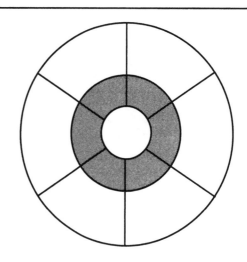

www.scholastic.co.uk

Mystery number crossword

♣ Spell out the mystery number (1 down) by using the clues.

Clues

1 Days in a week.

2 Nine less than twenty.

3 Double six.

4 Two times two times two.

5 The difference between nineteen and twenty.

6 Four fours.

7 Twenty-five less three less twelve.

8 Nine divided by three.

9 Two add six add one.

♣ Now make up a clue for the mystery number.

NO FUSS
PHOTOCOPIABLE

SCHOLASTIC
www.scholastic.co.uk

Times bingo

You can play this game with one or more friends.
You will need: two dice (numbered 1 to 6), some card, pens or pencils and some counters.

♣ Make your own bingo cards.

• Draw a 4 × 3 grid on to a piece of card.

• Colour any one section in each row. Perhaps like this:

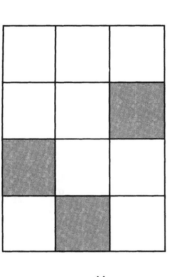

• Choose any nine numbers from the grid below to complete your card.

• Try to make your card different from your friend's card.

♣ The players take turns to:
• roll both dice and work out the product of the two numbers, for example: 4 × 5 = 20;
• cover that square if it is on their bingo card.

♣ The winner is the first player to cover all their bingo card numbers.

♣ Are some numbers a better choice for your card than others?

♣ Invent some other multiplication games using the dice and your bingo cards. What are the rules?

1	2	3	4	5	6
8	9	10	12	15	16
18	20	24	25	30	36

■ SCHOLASTIC
www.scholastic.co.uk

NO FUSS
PHOTOCOPIABLE

Name _____

Hangmaths

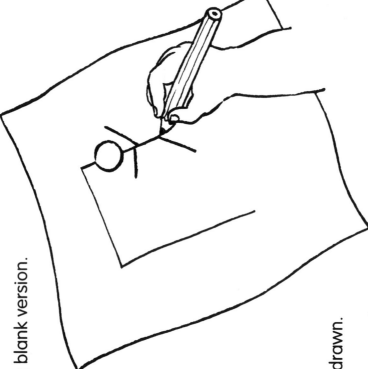

In this game you have to discover all the numbers in a secret sum without being 'hanged'.

✤ One player secretly makes up a sum and shows the other player a blank version.
For example, for:

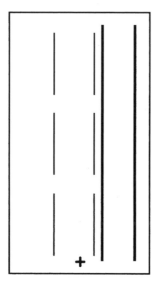

show

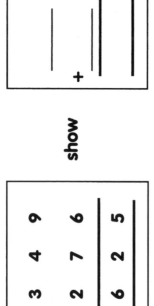

✤ Then the other player selects any column and any digit and asks a question such as, 'Is there a 2 in the tens column?'

✤ If there is, the digit is filled in. If not, part of the hangman picture is drawn.

✤ A player can win by managing to 'hang' his opponent, or by working out the whole sum correctly before being 'hanged'.

✤ Then the winner has to choose the next secret sum.

✤ Try the same activity using four and five-digit numbers.

Name _____

Sequences

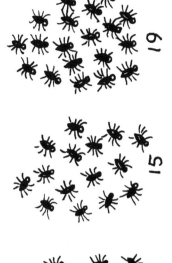
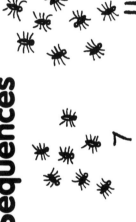
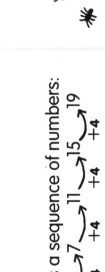

Here is a sequence of numbers:

$$3 \xrightarrow{+4} 7 \xrightarrow{+4} 11 \xrightarrow{+4} 15 \xrightarrow{+4} 19$$

The numbers increase by 4 each time.

✳ Complete each of the following sequences for a total of eight terms altogether.

1	6	11	16	21	26
2	72	65	58	51	44
3	10	13	17	20	24
4	60	55	53	48	46
5	$\frac{3}{4}$	1	$1\frac{1}{4}$	$1\frac{1}{2}$	$1\frac{3}{4}$
6	$2\frac{1}{2}$	$3\frac{1}{2}$	$4\frac{1}{2}$	$5\frac{1}{2}$	$6\frac{1}{2}$
7	18	$17\frac{1}{4}$	$16\frac{1}{2}$	$15\frac{3}{4}$	15
8	$\frac{5}{10}$	$\frac{7}{10}$	$1\frac{1}{10}$	$1\frac{3}{10}$	$1\frac{7}{10}$
9	1.0	1.2	1.4	1.6	1.8
10	20.3	19.8	19.3	18.8	18.3
11	18.5	18.25	18.0	17.75	17.5
12	1.32	1.44	1.56	1.68	1.8

SCHOLASTIC
www.scholastic.co.uk

NO FUSS PHOTOCOPIABLE

1, 2, 3, 4

1 Using just the digits 1, 2, 3 and 4 and the operations +, −, × and ÷, find a way to make each of the numbers from 1 to 10 on your calculator.

2 You must use each digit once, but only once, in any number sentence. You can mix the operations.

3 Record how you made each of the numbers, you may find more than one way. One example is given to help you.

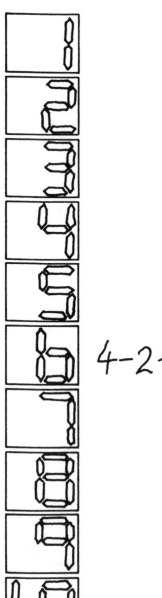

$4 - 2 + 3 + 1 = 6$

SCHOLASTIC
www.scholastic.co.uk

Press here

◆ How many ways can you get 36 on the calculator by using six key presses? One has been done for you.

◆ Record them in the blanks below.

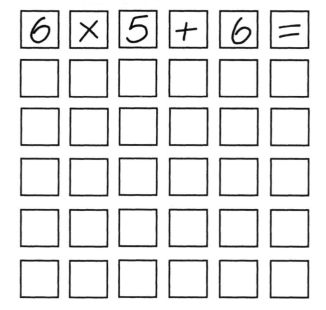

◆ What about 20 with five key presses?

◆ Choose a target number and number of key presses for someone else to try.

Two 2s

◆ Using 2 two times and +, –, × or ÷, which numbers can you make?
◆ Record what you did here. One example is given.

$$2 + 2 = 4$$

◆ Now do the same using **three 3s** and record what you did here.

◆ Explore ideas using, for example, two 2s and two 3s. You must use all four numbers each time. One example is given.

$2 + 2 + 3 \times 3 = 13$

NO FUSS PHOTOCOPIABLE

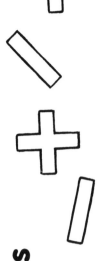

Starting numbers

♣ Solve these number puzzles and find the starting number for each.

Starting number _____

I multiplied by 4, subtracted 16 and divided by 7. The result was 12.

Starting number _____

I doubled it and added 11. Then I multiplied it by 5 and added 4. I ended up with 89.

Starting number _____

I doubled it, took away 6, divided by 3 and the answer was 10.

Starting number _____

I subtracted 12 and divided by 3, then I halved it and added 5. The result was 20.

♣ Now try making up some puzzles of your own, check them through and try them on a friend.

SCHOLASTIC
www.scholastic.co.uk

How close can you get?

Use your calculator to help

14

34

29

12

18

❖ What **whole number** does each of these numbers have to be multiplied by to get as close as possible to 100?

❖ Use decimals to get closer still. How close can you get?

PHOTOCOPIABLE

Television times

♣ Do you think there is more sport or more news shown on television?

♣ Which channel do you think devotes the most time to music?

♣ Use a television programmes guide to collect information about television broadcasting for a week. Sort the programmes into categories, for example, sport, music, drama and news.

♣ Work out the average time (in minutes) for each category, shown by each channel, on a weekday and a non-weekday. Present your findings in the form of pie charts. Each chart should show a 24-hour period.

♣ Were your answers to the questions at the top of the page correct? Can you tell just by looking at the pie charts?

Name _____

Ordering equipment

At the start of every school year, we need to check that each class has got everything that will be needed.

◆ Complete the checklist below for a class which has 27 children in it.

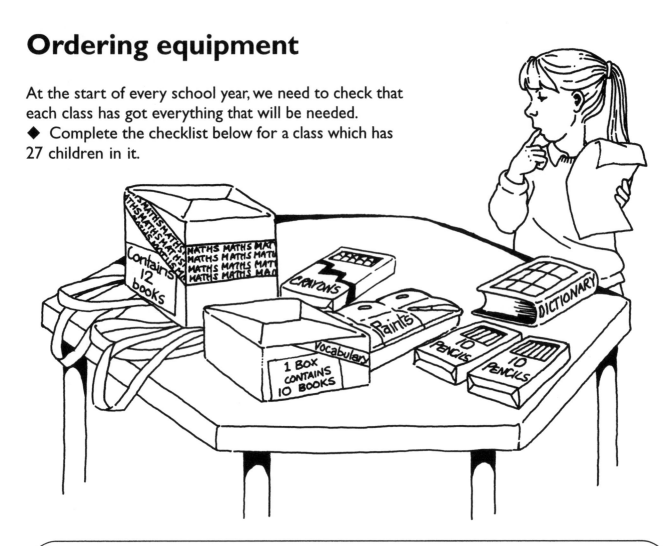

Checklist	How many to order
• Tables (each can seat six pupils)	_____
• Vocabulary books	_____
• Packets of crayons (1 packet between 3 pupils)	_____
• Packets of pencils (3 pencils for each pupil)	_____
• Mathematics books	_____
• Team bands in four colours for PE	_____
• Dictionaries (1 shared between 2 pupils)	_____
• Watercolour paintboxes (1 shared between 4 pupils)	_____

◆ Will there be spares of anything? Why?

SCHOLASTIC
www.scholastic.co.uk

Table repeats

The digital root of a number is the single digit you eventually get to by repeatedly adding together the digits in the original number.

For example: if the number is 24, adding the digits 2 + 4 gives a digital root of 6; or 98 gives 9 + 8 = 17, so 1 + 7 gives a digital root of 8.

❖ Investigate the times tables to see if there are any patterns in the digital roots of the answers. Try the three times and six times tables first.

❖ Look at the other times tables in the same way.

Three times table

Number	Digital root
3	3
6	6
9	9
12	3
15	6
18	9

❖ Does the pattern continue?

Six times table

Number	Digital root
6	6
12	3
18	9
24	6

❖ Does the pattern continue?

Three jumps to 100

✣ In this activity, you must use three jumps to reach 100. You may start at any number from 1 to 100 and you may use any of these signs: +, −, ÷, ×. For example:

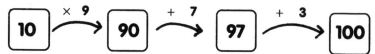

You may only use a single digit for the operation. No two-digit numbers are allowed.

✣ Try to find a way to make 100 for every starting number from 1 to 100.

✣ What patterns do you notice?

1	2	3	4	5	6	7	8	9	10
11	12	13	14	15	16	17	18	19	20
21	22	23	24	25	26	27	28	29	30
31	32	33	34	35	36	37	38	39	40
41	42	43	44	45	46	47	48	49	50
51	52	53	54	55	56	57	58	59	60
61	62	63	64	65	66	67	68	69	70
71	72	73	74	75	76	77	78	79	80
81	82	83	84	85	86	87	88	89	90
91	92	93	94	95	96	97	98	99	100

NO FUSS
PHOTOCOPIABLE

SCHOLASTIC
www.scholastic.co.uk

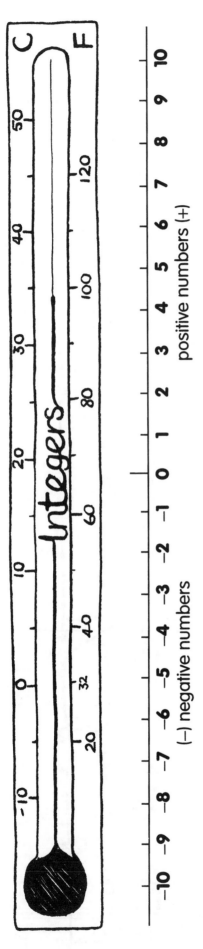

-10 -9 -8 -7 -6 -5 -4 -3 -2 -1 0 1 2 3 4 5 6 7 8 9 10

(–) negative numbers   positive numbers (+)

This is an integer number line. Numbers on the right-hand side of the line are positive (+) numbers. Numbers on the left-hand side of the line are negative (–) numbers.

If you start at –3 and jump four spaces in a positive direction you land on +1. If you start on +2 and jump six spaces in a negative direction you land on –4.

♣ Use the integer number line to help you to solve these problems.

1 Start at –5 and jump eight spaces in a positive direction. Where do you land?

2 Start at +3 and jump six spaces in a negative direction. Where do you land?

3 Moving in a positive direction, complete this number sequence: –8, –5, –2, ____, ____, ____.

Positive and negative numbers are used on a Celsius thermometer scale to show temperatures above and below freezing point (0°C).

♣ Use a thermometer to help you to work out these temperature problems.

4 By how many degrees has the temperature risen, if the 9 am reading is –3°C and the 2 pm reading is 4°C?

5 By how many degrees has the temperature fallen, if the 9 am reading is 2°C and the 2 pm reading is –6°C?

6 Find the average of these daily temperatures taken during December: 3°C, –2°C, 2°C, 5°C.

♣ Now use the number line to make up some similar sums of your own for a friend to try.

■SCHOLASTIC
www.scholastic.co.uk

NO FUSS
PHOTOCOPIABLE

0
1
1
2
3
5
8
13
21
34
55
89

Fibonacci

Almost 800 years ago, an Italian called Leonardo Fibonacci created the number sequence shown in the box opposite. Each number is made by adding the two numbers which come before.

♣ Keep on adding numbers to the Fibonacci sequence.

♣ Now put a line under any number in the sequence. The total of all the numbers above the line is equal to one less than the second number below the line. Try this a few times.

♣ Here is another activity.
• Take any three numbers in the sequence.
• Multiply the middle number by itself. Then multiply the first and third numbers together.
• Try this a number of times. Do the answers have something in common?

NO FUSS PHOTOCOPIABLE

SCHOLASTIC
www.scholastic.co.uk

Name _____

The birthday party

♣ Tom is having a birthday party.
He has invited four friends.
He has £6.50 to spend.
♣ These are the things he needs
to buy for each person:

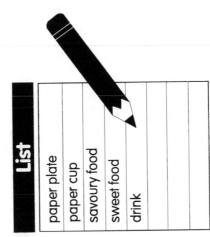

List	
paper plate	
paper cup	
savoury food	
sweet food	
drink	

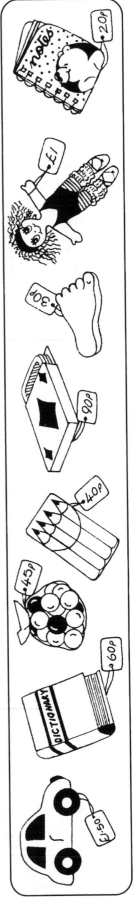

♣ He also needs to buy a prize for each of four games. Make a shopping list for him from the items shown.

♣ If you were giving a party, what would you buy? How much would it cost?

Book fair

You may need a calculator.

ATLAS £1·95

SHORT STORIES 1 £1·50

CREEPY TALES £3·50

PUZZLE BOOK 65P

BOOK OF KNOWLEDGE £3·99

SHORT STORIES 2 £1·50

TREE SPOTTER 95P

FOOTBALL FUN BOOK £2·25

STICKER BOOK 1 75P

FAIRY STORIES £2·50

STICKER BOOK 2 75P

At the book fair each child has £5.00 to spend.

✤ Joanne buys two books for exactly £5.00. Which books are they?

✤ Sam buys four books and still has change. Which books are they?

✤ Ben buys the most expensive book and the least expensive book. How much change has Ben?

✤ How could Tony, Ajay and Siu Yin spend their money? Decide which books they could buy and how much change they will have. Each child chooses a different selection, but the fair has more than one of each book.

NO FUSS PHOTOCOPIABLE

■ SCHOLASTIC
www.scholastic.co.uk

Lose or gain?

✤ The Post Office only had 10p coins in the till. The cashier decided that the fairest way to cash postal orders would be to give each person their amount to the nearest 10p. So Leah will receive 40p. What will the others receive?

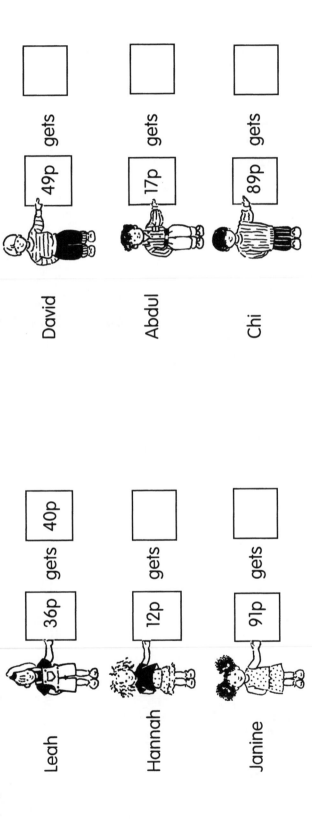

Leah | 36p gets 40p

Hannah | 12p gets ☐

Janine | 91p gets ☐

David | 49p gets ☐

Abdul | 17p gets ☐

Chi | 89p gets ☐

✤ Who will gain the most?

✤ Suppose the Post Office only had 5p coins in its till and paid each customer to the nearest 5p. Write down what each person would get.

Name _____

Link amounts

Each amount of money below has been shown in 3 different ways.
✤ Join each of the amounts that are the same, using different colours. The first one has been done for you.

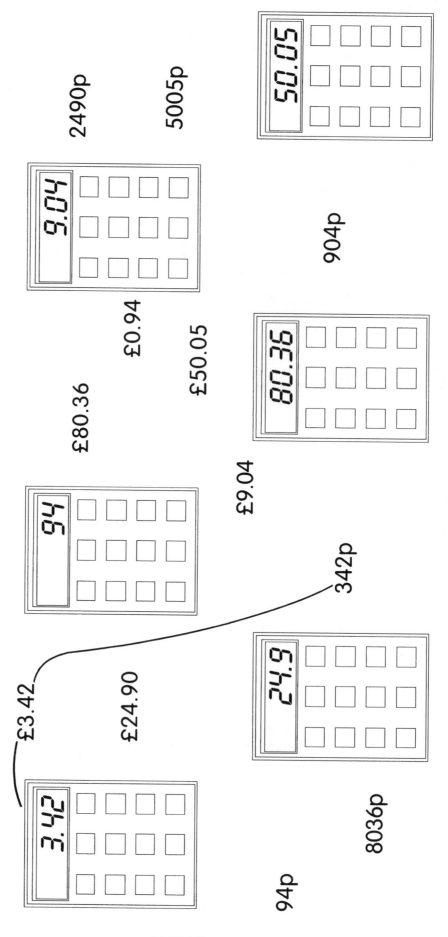

2490p

5005p

£0.94

£80.36

£50.05

£9.04

904p

342p

£3.42

£24.90

94p

8036p

✤ Set up some similar problems for other people to solve. Don't forget to put the amounts in the calculator displays.

■SCHOLASTIC
www.scholastic.co.uk

Coin corners

You must use the same single coin at each corner to make the
centre amount. Like this:

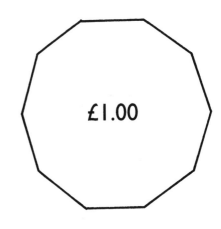

£1.00

◆ Write in the coin values at the corners.

◆ Try these in the same way.

£1.20

12p

£1.00

24p

30p

35p

◆ Some are impossible, which ones? **Why?** _____

_____

◆ Could you do any of the 'impossibles' with two coins of your choice at each corner?

◆ Make up some more puzzles like these for someone else to try.

Coins ©The Royal Mint

Christmas cards

(a) 15p each   (b) 18p each   (c) 15p each

(d) 20p each   (e) 22p each   (f) 25p each

1 You can spend up to £2 on Christmas cards. Which ones will you choose?

2 Choose three different assortments to go in boxes that will sell for £1.50.

3 Choose a dozen (12) cards for a selection box containing at least three different designs. What would be the price of the most expensive and least expensive box?

◆ Write your choices here.

1

2

3

SCHOLASTIC
www.scholastic.co.uk

Name _____

Bus conductor

The bus conductor does not want to have a lot of coins to count at the end of the day, so he gives passengers their change using **as many coins as possible**.

◆ How could he give these amounts of change? Remember that by law he can only give up to 20p worth of 1p and 2p coins at a time.

- 15p

- 20p

- 25p

- 27p

- 32p

- 68p

- 75p

Name _____

Lunch time

A game for two or three players.

You will need: a pencil and paper for each player for working out and the 'Lunch time' cards copied on to card and cut out.

1 Your aim is to be the first player to collect and show to the other players a complete meal of:
- a drink;
- a main course;
- vegetables;
- a pudding.

This scores 1 point.
If the total cost is £2 or less, score 5 bonus points.

2 Shuffle the cards, deal out four to each player and place the rest in a pile face down.

3 In turn, take the top card from the pile, look at it and decide whether to keep it or put it in a discard pile.
If you keep it, you must discard a different one from your hand.
Players can only have four cards in their hand at a time.

4 The round ends when a player puts down a complete meal.

5 Play five rounds.

Coffee 30p

Cod in batter £1.00

Baked beans 30p

Yoghurt 50p

NO FUSS PHOTOCOPIABLE

SCHOLASTIC
www.scholastic.co.uk

Lunch-time playing cards 1

Peas
35p

Baked beans
30p

Chips
40p

Burger
£0.90

Cod in batter
£1.00

Pizza
£0.75

Apple pie
45p

Ice-cream
35p

Sausages
£0.80

SCHOLASTIC
www.scholastic.co.uk

Name _____

Lunch-time playing cards 2

Yoghurt
35p

Chocolate
mousse
50p

Fruit salad
55p

Tea
25p

Coffee
30p

Cola
25p

Lemonade
20p

Orange juice
25p

Sweetcorn
30p

NO FUSS
PHOTOCOPIABLE

SCHOLASTIC
www.scholastic.co.uk

Name _____

Babysitting

This table shows the times Janine has babysat during November.

November

Name	Date	Start time	Finish time	Total time Rounded up	Money earned
Hunter	06.11.95	18.00	21.30		
Stephens	08.11.95	17.30	22.45		
MacLeod	10.11.95	09.45	12.37		
Jones	10.11.95	20.15	00.15		
Hunter	15.11.95	09.00	15.21		
Hunter	16.11.95	09.00	20.18		
MacLeod	21.11.95	16.40	17.54		
Jones	27.11.95	17.15	23.17		
Jones	28.11.95	17.15	23.55		
Hunter	30.11.95	08.30	14.36		
				Total earnings	

✤ Complete the table by working out how long each job took and how much Janine earned.

She charges £2.50 per hour plus 50p for each extra quarter hour.

All times are rounded up to the nearest quarter hour. For example, if she worked 2 hours 17 minutes she would charge for 2 hours 30 minutes.

✤ How much did each family pay?

● Hunter _____ ● Stephens _____

● MacLeod _____ ● Jones _____

✤ Which family is her best client? _____

Why? _____

■SCHOLASTIC
www.scholastic.co.uk

Name _____

Shopping

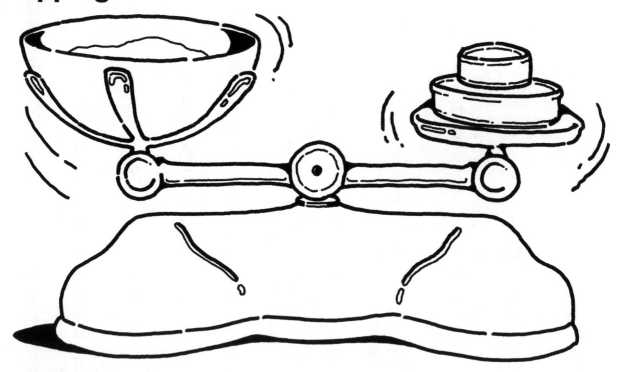

The stallholder's scales only tell him the 'weight'. He is making a table
to help him with the prices.

◆ Fill in the prices.

Weight	Coleslaw 15p for 100g	Cream cheese 53p for 100g	Ham 75p for 100g	Roast beef £3.00 for 100g
100g				
200g				
300g				
400g				
500g				
600g				
700g				
800g				
900g				
1kg				

NO FUSS PHOTOCOPIABLE

SCHOLASTIC
www.scholastic.co.uk

Name _____

Sharing the bill

Here is a collection of bills from two different restaurants.

A The Peacock Restaurant — Your total bill comes to £98.42 — Service charge not included

B GREENS FISH RESTAURANT — £86.49 — Service charge at 10% has been added

C The Peacock Restaurant — £204.86 — Service charge not included

D GREENS FISH RESTAURANT — £49.89 — Service charge at 10% has been added

E The Peacock Restaurant — £120.56 — Service charge not included

F The Peacock Restaurant — £69.51 — Service charge not included

G GREENS FISH RESTAURANT — £149.50 — Service charge at 10% has been added

Remember
The bills from Greens Fish Restaurant include service charge, but the bills from The Peacock do not. You may wish to take this into consideration when sharing out the costs. When service charge is not included people usually leave a tip. You will have to decide how much to leave.

♣ Each bill is to be shared evenly by the following groups of people.
♣ How much will each individual have to pay?

Bill A – 5 people _____
Bill B – 4 people _____
Bill C – 10 people _____

Bill D – 3 people _____
Bill E – 4 people _____
Bill F – 5 people _____
Bill G –10 people _____

■ SCHOLASTIC
www.scholastic.co.uk

NO FUSS PHOTOCOPIABLE

Cold days

Some children recorded the outside temperatures every day for a week.
Here are the results:

Monday 10th	9°C
Tuesday 11th	8°C
Wednesday 12th	7°C
Thursday 13th	7°C
Friday 14th	4°C

During the following week, the weather became much colder. Some days the temperature dropped below 0° Celsius. The children noted by how much the temperature had fallen compared with the same day of the previous week.

Monday 17th	6°C less
Tuesday 18th	8°C less
Wednesday 19th	8°C less
Thursday 20th	9°C less
Friday 21st	7°C less

✤ Complete this table to show the temperature recordings for both weeks:

Day	Date	Temp	Date	Temp
Monday	10th	9°C	17th	3°C
Tuesday	11th		18th	
Wednesday	12th		19th	
Thursday	13th		20th	
Friday	14th		21st	

Draw a graph of the temperatures for both weeks.

NO FUSS
PHOTOCOPIABLE

■ SCHOLASTIC
www.scholastic.co.uk

Name _____

Number of children in class	Can make teams of 2 exactly	Can make teams of 5 exactly	Can make teams of 10 exactly
10	5	2	1
11			
12			
13			
14			
15			
16			
17			
18			
19			
20			
21			
22			
23			
24			
25			
26			
27			
28			
29			
30			

PE teams

There are thirty children in the class. They need to split up into teams for different games in their PE lessons. Sometimes children are away, so the class is smaller.

✤ Decide for each number of children left in the class whether they could split into teams of 2, 5 or 10 without anyone being left out.

✤ Fill in the table, saying how many teams can be made. One has been done for you.

SCHOLASTIC
www.scholastic.co.uk

Name _____

Flaming June

Class 3 kept a record of the weather in June and recorded it using these symbols:

sunny   rainy   cloudy

Here is their weather chart:

Sunday	6 rainy	13 sunny	20 sunny	27 sunny
Monday	7 rainy	14 sunny	21 rainy	28 sunny
Tuesday	1 sunny	8 rainy	15 sunny	22 cloudy	29 cloudy
Wednesday	2 sunny	9 cloudy	16 sunny	23 sunny	30 sunny
Thursday	3 sunny	10 rainy	17 rainy	24 sunny
Friday	4 cloudy	11 cloudy	18 sunny	25 cloudy
Saturday	5 cloudy	12 rainy	19 sunny	26 sunny

♣ From Class 3's weather chart, count the number of:

- sunny days _____
- cloudy days _____
- rainy days _____
- days altogether _____

♣ Make your own weather chart for a month using Class 3's symbols.

Sunday						
Monday						
Tuesday						
Wednesday						
Thursday						
Friday						
Saturday						

NO FUSS
PHOTOCOPIABLE

SCHOLASTIC
www.scholastic.co.uk

Name _____

Favourite sports

Class 5 have done a survey. They asked every child in the class about their favourite sport. They recorded the data and made a graph.

football	⊬Ⴕ IIII
judo	III
rounders	⊬Ⴕ
swimming	⊬Ⴕ III
tennis	II

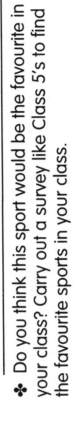

* How many children are there in the class?

* What is the favourite sport?

* Do you think this sport would be the favourite in your class? Carry out a survey like Class 5's to find the favourite sports in your class.

	football	judo	rounders	swimming	tennis
10					
9					
8					
7					
6					
5					
4					
3					
2					
1					
0					

SCHOLASTIC
www.scholastic.co.uk

Fixture list

Four football teams decided to form a league: West United, East Rovers, North Town and South Albion. In one season, each team will play all the other teams twice, once at home and once away.

❖ How many matches will each team play?

❖ How many matches will be played altogether?

Another club, Compass Athletic, decides to join the league.
❖ How many matches will they have to play?

❖ How many matches will now be played altogether?

The English Premier League has 22 teams.
❖ How many matches will, say, Manchester United play in the league each season?

❖ How many matches will be played altogether in the Premier League in one season?

NO FUSS PHOTOCOPIABLE

SCHOLASTIC
www.scholastic.co.uk

Name _____

Tallying

Tallying is a simple system which can be used to collect large amounts of data easily. In a tally system:

I	means one item,
II	means two items,
III	means three items,
IIII	means four items,
IIII̶	means five items.....

These tally charts show the number of people using a pedestrian crossing during three periods in a day.

8.00 am / 9.00 am

| Adults | IIII̶ IIII̶ IIII̶ IIII̶ IIII̶ IIII̶ IIII̶ II |
| Children | IIII̶ IIII̶ IIII̶ I |

1.00 pm / 2.00 pm

| Adults | IIII̶ IIII̶ IIII̶ IIII̶ IIII̶ IIII̶ IIII̶ IIII̶ IIII̶ IIII |
| Children | IIII̶ IIII̶ I |

6.00 pm / 7.00 pm

| Adults | IIII̶ IIII̶ IIII̶ IIII̶ IIII̶ IIII̶ IIII̶ IIII̶ |
| Children | IIII̶ II |

✦ Convert the information shown into graphs.

✦ Now answer these questions.
* How many children use the crossing altogether?

* How many adults use the crossing altogether?

* Which time do most adults use the crossing?

* Which time do most children use the crossing?

* Which time is the busiest overall?

✦ Discuss the reasons for your answers.

SCHOLASTIC
www.scholastic.co.uk

Heads and tails

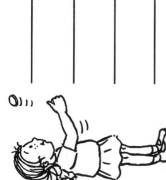

You will need: a coin.

When a coin is tossed it is equally likely to come down 'heads' or 'tails'.

✤ Work with a partner and predict how many 'heads' and how many 'tails' you would expect if you tossed the coin ten times. If you tossed the coin 100 times, how many 'heads' and how many 'tails' would you expect?

✤ Now test this out. Toss the coin ten times and ask your partner to record the results in the first column.

✤ How many times did you get 'heads' and how many times did you get 'tails'?

✤ Now ask your partner to toss the coin ten times while you record the results in the second column. Are your results similar?

✤ Increase the number of times you toss the coin. Try 20, 50 and 100 times. Record your results.

✤ What do you notice about the results?

Toss	Results	
1		
2		
3		
4		
5		
6		
7		
8		
9		
10		

NO FUSS PHOTOCOPIABLE

SCHOLASTIC www.scholastic.co.uk

Happy birthday

❖ What is the average age of the children in your class (in years and months)?

_____

❖ Are you above or below the average age and by how much?

_____

❖ How far above the average age is the oldest class member?

_____

❖ How far below the average age is the youngest class member?

_____

❖ How many, if any, are exactly the average age?

_____

Watching television

♣ What was the most popular viewing time last night amongst the children in your class?
To answer this question you will need to collect information from each person in the class.
This table may help you :

Time	Number of children watching TV
4:00 – 4:30	
4:30 – 5:00	
5:00 – 5:30	
5:30 – 6:00	
6:00 – 6:30	
6:30 – 7:00	
7:00 – 7:30	
7:30 – 8:00	
8:00 – 8:30	
8:30 – 9:00	
9:00 – 9:30	
9:30 – 10:00	

♣ Construct a graph below to show your results.

♣ Can you suggest why some times are more popular?
♣ Would a similar graph for tonight look the same?

NO FUSS PHOTOCOPIABLE

SCHOLASTIC
www.scholastic.co.uk

Mini sports

A group of children took part in a mini sports session. They each kept
their own score card, and are now ready to award points for each event:

- 5 points for first place;
- 4 points for second;
- 3 points for third;
- 2 points for fourth;
- 1 point for fifth.

◆ Place the results in order for each event in the spaces at the
bottom of the page and award the points.

Name: Jo
Long jump   1·90m
Standing jump   2·10 m
Bean bag throw   9·65m
Balance beam walk   3·05m
Hopped in 30secs   20·03m

Name: Sam
Long jump   2·10m
Standing jump   2·05m
Bean bag throw   9·45m
Balance beam walk   3·35 m
Hopped in 30secs   20·30m

Name: Jill
Long jump   2·05m
Standing jump   1·19m
Bean bag throw   8·95m
Balance beam walk   3·65m
Hopped in 30secs   21·35m

Name: Tom
Long jump   2·00m
Standing jump   1·90m
Bean bag throw   8·65m
Balance beam walk   3·68m
Hopped in 30secs   19·95m

Name: Faarea
Long jump   2·15m
Standing jump   1·98m
Bean bag throw   9·05m
Balance beam walk   3·78m
Hopped in 30secs   20·35m

Name: David
Long jump   1·75m
Standing jump   1·95m
Bean bag throw   9·15m
Balance beam walk   3·60m
Hopped in 30secs   23·15m

Results

	Long jump	Standing jump	Bean bag throw	Balance beam walk	30sec hop
1st	_____	_____	_____	_____	_____
2nd	_____	_____	_____	_____	_____
3rd	_____	_____	_____	_____	_____
4th	_____	_____	_____	_____	_____
5th	_____	_____	_____	_____	_____

◆ The overall winner is _____ because _____

_____

Name _____

Pie charts

The **pie chart** is another way of showing information.

This pie chart shows how children travel to school.

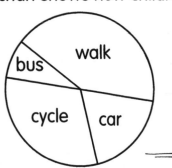

❧ Which is the most popular way to travel?

❧ Which is the least popular?

❧ Complete the table below to show how you spend your day.
The figures are the total number of hours spent doing each activity.

	school	playing	watching TV	eating	bed	other things
Jo	7	2	4	1	8	2
Me						

❧ Use both sets of figures to complete the pie charts to show
how you and Jo use your time.

My day:

Jo's day:

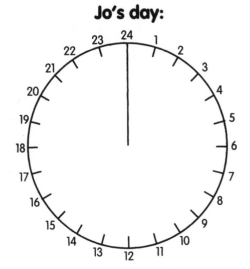

SCHOLASTIC
www.scholastic.co.uk

Name _____

New shoes

In interpreting data, the words **range**, **median** and **mode** are often used. The **range** is calculated by finding the difference between the highest and lowest number in the data. The **median** is the middle point, the **mode** is the most popular item and the **mean** is the average value.

These are the numbers of each different size of men's shoes sold in a shoe shop during one Saturday:

Men's shoe sizes	7	7½	8	8½	9	9½	10	10½	11	11½	12
Number of customers	5	1	12	18	24	15	19	14	8	6	3

✤ Record the information about shoe sales shown in the table above on the graph opposite.

✤ What is the range of sizes? _____

✤ What is the median size? _____

✤ What is the mode? _____

✤ What is the mean? _____

✤ How might this data help the shoe shop manager?

NO FUSS
PHOTOCOPIABLE

Venn diagrams

This is a type of graph called a **Venn diagram**. It shows a number of sets of information together.

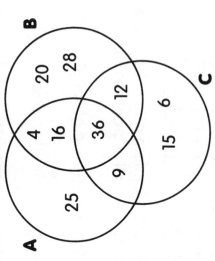

In this Venn diagram the numbers used are: 4, 6, 9, 12, 15, 16, 20, 25, 28 and 36. They are divided into three sets:

A = (square numbers)
B = (multiples of 4)
C = (multiples of 3)

(A square number is made by multiplying a number by itself, for example 5 × 5 = 25. A multiple of, say, 4 is any number made by multiplying by 4. So 20 is a multiple of 4, since 4 × 5 = 20.)

❖ Use the information in the Venn diagram to answer the following questions.

• Which number is a square number only? _____

• Which numbers are multiples of 4 only? _____

• Which numbers are multiples of 3 only? _____

• Which numbers are multiples of 4 and square numbers? _____

• Which numbers are multiples of 3 and square numbers? _____

• Which numbers are multiples of 3, 4 and square numbers? _____

NO FUSS
PHOTOCOPIABLE

■SCHOLASTIC
www.scholastic.co.uk

Curved graphs

✤ Complete the table below and then mark the points on the graph.

Length of side of square	1	2	3	4	5	6
Area of square						

✤ Join the points with a smooth curve.

✤ Use the graph to find the areas of squares with sides:
- $2\frac{1}{2}$ cm;
- $3\frac{1}{2}$ cm;
- $4\frac{1}{2}$ cm.

✤ Find the length of the side of a square which has an area of:
- 5cm;
- 15cm;
- 20cm.

✤ Check your answers by using a calculator.

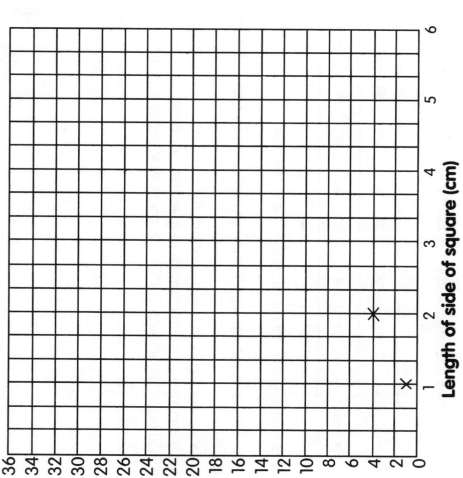

Length of side of square (cm)

Area of square (cm²)

Name _____

Production costs

This table shows the production costs of a new line of toy.

Number produced	100	200	300	400	500	600	700	800	900	1000	1100	1200	1300	1400
Cost per item (in pence)	50	48	46	44	42	40	38	36	34	32	30	28	26	24

❖ Construct a graph to represent this information.

To meet with a minimum profit margin, production costs of not more than forty pence per item have to be achieved.

❖ Show on your graph the projected effects of production cost increases of (i) 20% and (ii) 40%.
For each increase, use the graph to give the approximate minimum number of items that would have to be produced each time to be within the minimum profit margins.

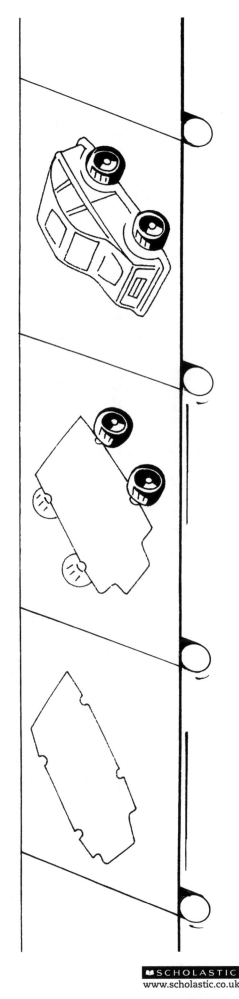

NO FUSS
PHOTOCOPIABLE

■SCHOLASTIC
www.scholastic.co.uk

Totals

1	2	3	4	5	6	7	8	9	10	11	12

♣ Throw two (1–6) dice together. Count the total number of spots and tick a box for that number on the table above.

♣ Keep throwing the dice until one column on the table is full. Which number was your most common total?

♣ ♣ List all the ways that you could have thrown the dice to get that total.

♣ ♣ ♣ Using a (1–6) and a (7–12) die, try the activity again. Make a new table to use with these dice.

Name _____

Fishy pictures

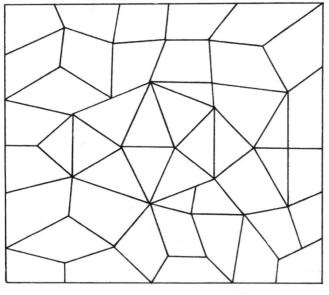

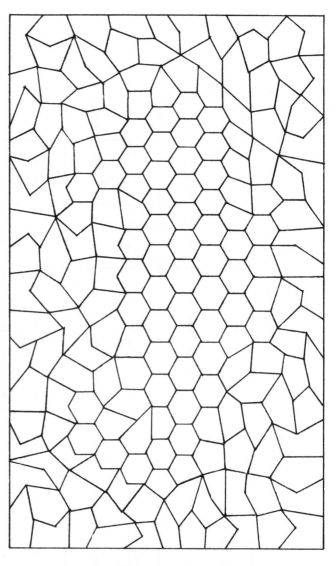

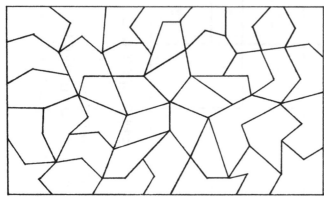

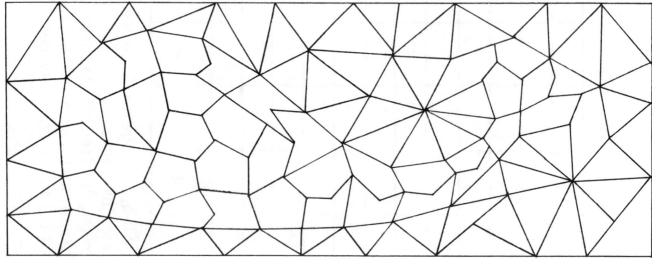

◆ Colour:
• triangles in blue;
• quadrilaterals in red;
• pentagons in green;
• hexagons in yellow.

◆ Find:
• a huge whale;
• a sea-horse;
• a fish;
• a starfish.

NO FUSS PHOTOCOPIABLE

Name _____

Shape tree

A set of three-dimensional shapes like these may help you:

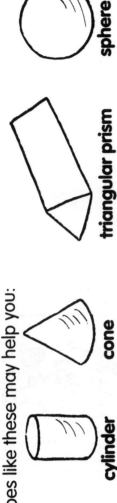

cube **cuboid** **cylinder** **cone** **triangular prism** **sphere**

✤ Complete this tree diagram using each of these shapes in turn. Write the name of the shape in all of the appropriate places on the diagram.

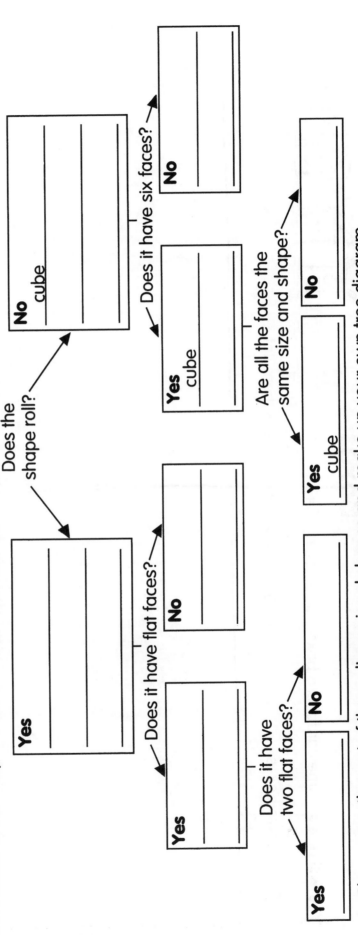

Does the shape roll?

Yes

No _____ cube

Does it have flat faces?

Yes

No

Does it have six faces?

Yes cube

No

Does it have two flat faces?

Yes

No

Are all the faces the same size and shape?

Yes cube

No

✤ Choose another set of three-dimensional shapes and make up your own tree diagram.

SCHOLASTIC
www.scholastic.co.uk

NO FUSS
PHOTOCOPIABLE

Boxes

You will need: some cardboard boxes, a pencil, a ruler.

✿ Choose two boxes.

✿ Open them out and press them flat.

✿ Draw their nets here:

✿ How are they different? _____

✿ How are the nets alike? _____

NO FUSS
PHOTOCOPIABLE

SCHOLASTIC
www.scholastic.co.uk

Name _____

Structures with cubes

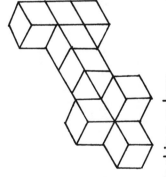

* Using interlocking cubes, make different structures with 10 cubes in each.

* Sort them into 2 sets, those that are symmetrical and those that are not.

* Where is the plane of symmetry?

* Have some shapes got more than one plane of symmetry?

* Try making other structures with more or fewer cubes and explore these ideas.

* Choose one of your structures and try to draw it.

Buried treasure

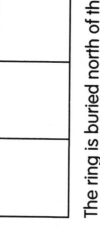

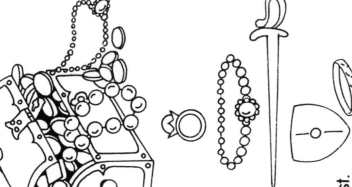

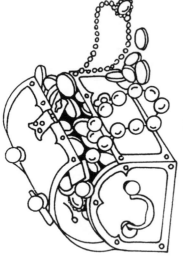

The ring is buried north of the treasure chest.

The necklace is buried east of the sword.

The bracelet is buried north-east of the coins.

The gold is buried south-east of the bracelet.

The sword is buried north-west of the shield.

The treasure chest is buried north-west of the crown.

✤ Find the treasure and the treasure chest and draw them in the correct spaces on the blank chart above.

The ring is buried north of the treasure chest.

The necklace is buried south of the treasure chest.

The sword is buried west of the treasure chest.

The shield is buried east of the treasure chest.

The bracelet is buried south-east of the treasure chest.

The gold coins are buried south-west of the treasure chest.

The crown is buried north-west of the treasure chest.

The gold bar is buried north-east of the treasure chest.

✤ By following these directions, draw the treasures around the treasure chest on the chart.

NO FUSS
PHOTOCOPIABLE

SCHOLASTIC
www.scholastic.co.uk

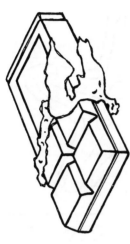

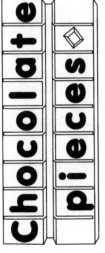

Chocolate pieces

These bars of chocolate have been broken up and mixed up.

❖ Carefully cut out each piece and put pieces of the same size together to make 3 complete bars. All the whole bars should be the same size.

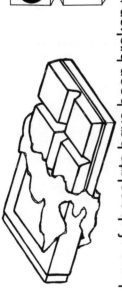

❖ Can you find different ways of making the 3 whole bars by mixing up the pieces?
❖❖ How would you record your results?

Name _____

Draw the other half

◆ Draw the other half of each of these sea creatures. Each half should match exactly.

◆ Find a partner. Each put your pencils on the dotted centre line in the same place. You lead, drawing half a symmetrical picture of a sea creature. Your partner should follow you, trying to draw the other half at the same time.

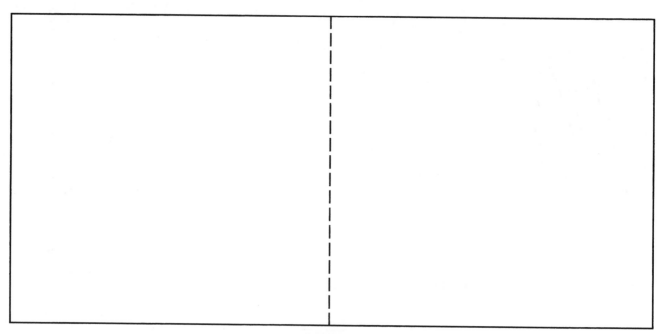

PHOTOCOPIABLE

SCHOLASTIC
www.scholastic.co.uk

Name _____

Lines of symmetry

◆ Cut out the shapes below.

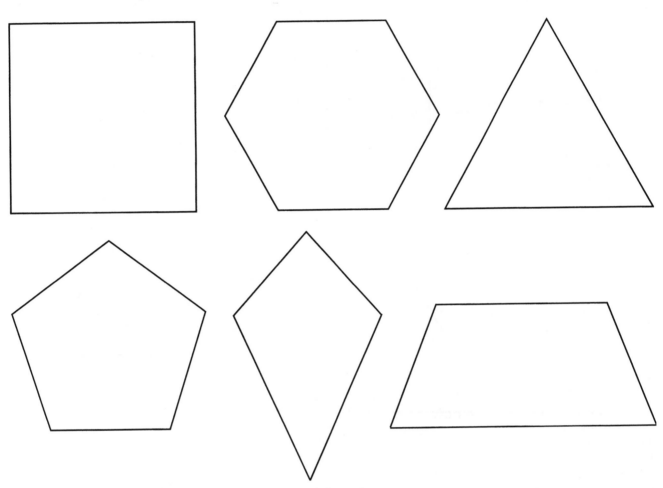

◆ How many ways can each shape be folded in half so that the edges match exactly?

These folds mark the 'line (or lines) of symmetry'.

◆ Draw in the lines of symmetry which you find on these smaller versions of the shapes above.

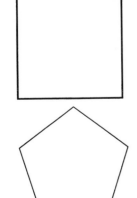
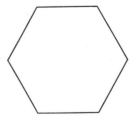
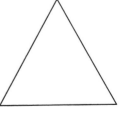

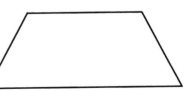

Name _____

Rotating a shape

◆ Cut out these shapes and match them to the outlines below.

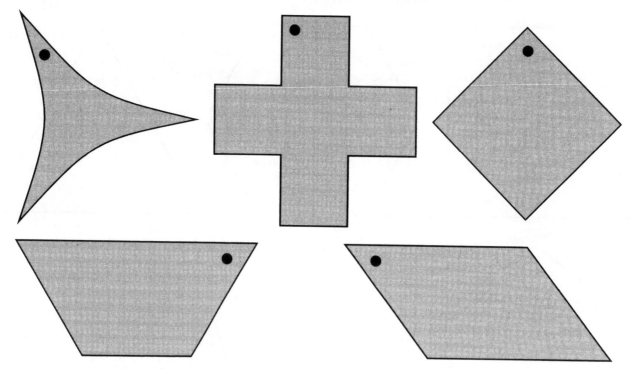

◆ How many ways will each shape fit into its outline without being turned over? Write how many ways in the small boxes.
The dots on the shapes are to help you to check where you started.

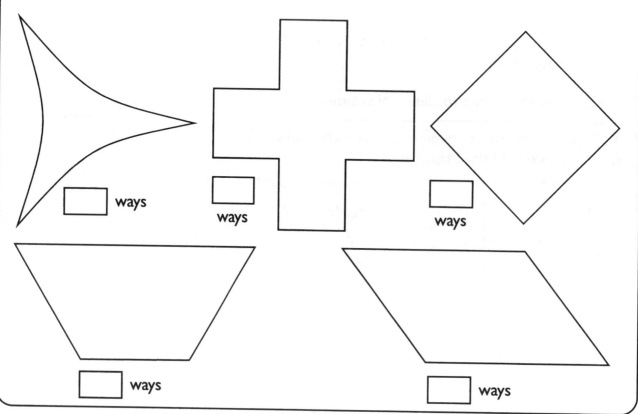

NO FUSS
PHOTOCOPIABLE

SCHOLASTIC
www.scholastic.co.uk

Symmetry patterns

◆ Choose a sheet of squared or spotty paper.
◆ Fold your chosen sheet of paper in half.
◆ Colour in a pattern on one half.
◆ Now open up the paper and colour in
the other side to make a symmetrical pattern.
◆ You could check the symmetry of your pattern with
a mirror.

◆ Now fold another sheet of squared or spotty paper
into quarters.
◆ Colour in one quarter.
◆ Unfold the sheet and colour in the other quarters
to produce a symmetrical pattern.

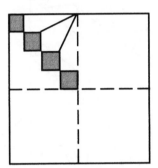

- -

Symmetry dominoes – the game

A game for two players.

You will need: the 'Symmetry dominoes' playing cards.

◆ Shuffle the dominoes and deal them so that you have four
cards each.
◆ Put the other cards face down in a pile between you.
◆ The dealer now turns over the top card on the pile
and places it face up to start a line of dominoes.
◆ The other person should then place one of their
cards next to it to make a symmetrical shape and then
take another card from the pile. (See example
opposite.)
◆ Take turns to add a domino from your hand to
make a line of symmetrical pictures. If you can't place a
card, take another from the pile anyway.
◆ If you can't place a card, take another card from the pile
anyway.
◆ Once the cards in the pile are gone, play until one person
wins by using all their dominoes!
◆ If no one can place a card, then the player with the fewest
dominoes in their hand is the winner.

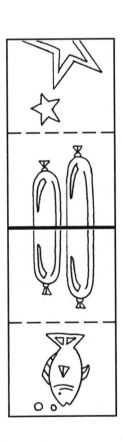

SCHOLASTIC
www.scholastic.co.uk

NO FUSS
PHOTOCOPIABLE

Name _____

Symmetry dominoes – 1

NO FUSS
PHOTOCOPIABLE

SCHOLASTIC
www.scholastic.co.uk

Name _____

Symmetry dominoes – 2

■SCHOLASTIC
www.scholastic.co.uk

NO FUSS
PHOTOCOPIABLE

Name _____

Spiral loops

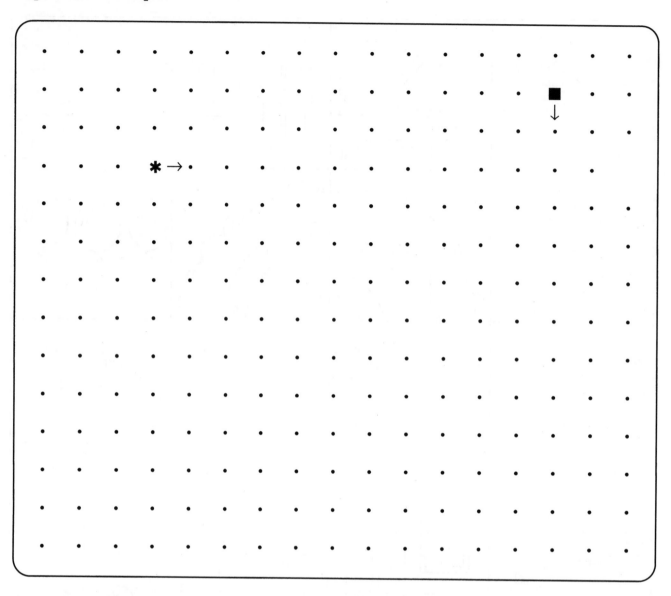

◆ Start at the **✳**.

◆ Follow the arrow and mark this route with a line as you go:

• 1 unit length forward, turn right;

• 2 units length forward, turn right;

• 3 units length forward, turn right;

• 1 unit length forward, turn right;

• 2 units length forward, turn right;

• 3 units length forward, turn right...;

• Repeat this until it seems sensible to stop!

◆ Now start at the **■** and begin by following the arrow.

◆ Turning right each time, use this pattern of numbers for the units of length to draw the lines: 3, 3, 1, 2, 3, 3, 1, 2 and so on.

◆ Now try a pattern of your own.

www.scholastic.co.uk

Name _____

Mystery picture

♣ Draw the picture by plotting the co-ordinates and joining each point to the next with a straight line.
1,0; 3,2; 3,5; 3,8; 5,10; 7,8; 7,5; 7,2; 9,0; 7,0; 7,1; 6,1; 6,0; 4,0; 4,1; 3,1; 3,0; join the last point to the first.

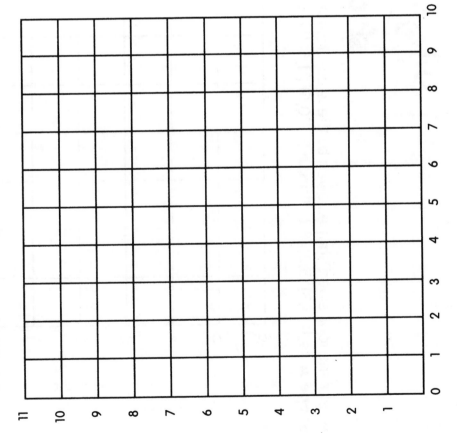

♣ Design your own picture. Write down the co-ordinates for it so that someone else could draw the picture from your instructions.

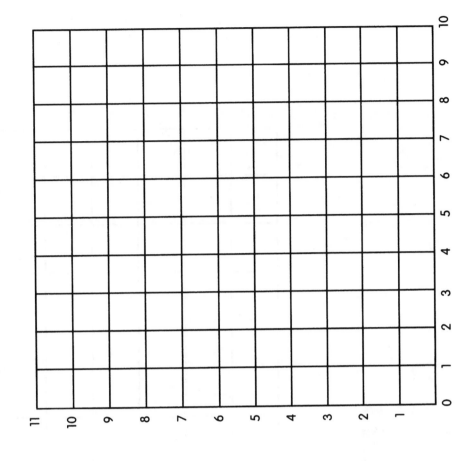

Name _____

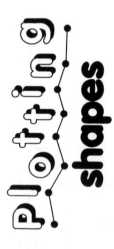

Plotting shapes

❖ Plot the four-sided shapes given by these co-ordinates.

Shape A (4,1) (5,3) (8,3) (8,1) **Shape B** (10,5) (11,5) (12,3) (10,3)

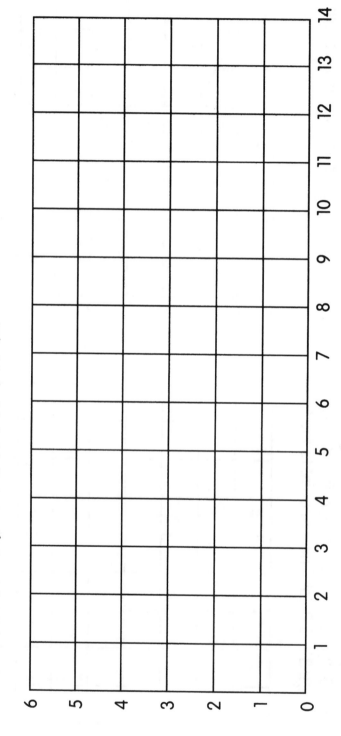

❖ If the sides of each shape are doubled in length, give the new set of co-ordinates for each.

❖ Plot the enlarged shapes.

❖ Work out roughly the area of each shape and make a statement about how the area of each new shape compares with the area of its original shape.

SCHOLASTIC
www.scholastic.co.uk

Cubes and cuboids

❖ Look at these drawings and estimate how many cubes you would require to make each cuboid.

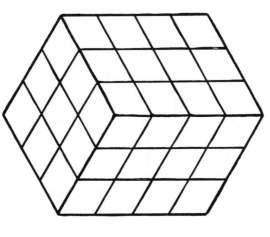

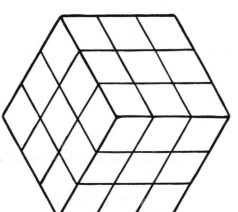

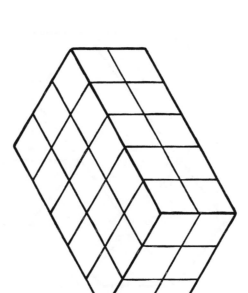

A ———————— B ———————— C ————————

❖ Use cubes to build each one and check your estimates.

❖❖ Take 24 cubes. How many different cuboids can be made with a volume of 24?

Name _____

Rotating shapes

3 Try some more shapes.

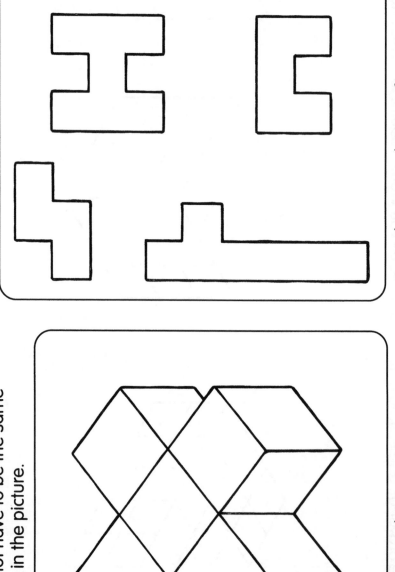

1 Make the following shape with linking cubes. It does not have to be the same size as the one in the picture.

2 Draw round your shape on paper. How many different ways can you fit your shape made of cubes onto your paper pattern? _____

4 Make some shapes of your own with cubes. Draw round them. How many ways can you fit your shapes onto their patterns?

5 Try the same activity with shapes from a set of two-dimensional (2-D) shapes.

NO FUSS
PHOTOCOPIABLE

SCHOLASTIC
www.scholastic.co.uk

Name _____

Guess the weight

❧ Which do you think weighs more - a shoe or a jumper?

❧ Get one of each and estimate their weight in grams.

❧ Fill in your estimates on the chart below. Now check your estimates.

❧ Try estimating the weight of some more pairs of objects and then check your estimates. Fill in the tables.

Object	Estimated weight	Weight in grams	Object	Estimated weight	Weight in grams
shoe			jumper		
ruler			scissors		
mug			plate		
spoon			fork		
book			dictionary		

❧ Choose 3 more pairs of objects, estimate and then check their weight.

Object	Estimated weight	Weight in grams	Object	Estimated weight	Weight in grams

❧ Does a shoe always weigh more than a jumper or a jumper always weigh more than a shoe? Test your theory.

📖 SCHOLASTIC
www.scholastic.co.uk

What could you use?

♣ Use some or all of them to help you fill in this table.

What to measure	Answer	Instrument used to measure with and reason for choosing it
The perimeter of the school playground.		
The length of the school hall.		
The height of your table.		
The width of your reading book.		
Your height.		
Your waist.		

♣ Could you have used more suitable equipment? If so, what?
♣♣ Ask a friend if they would have chosen to use the same equipment as you for each measurement you made. If not, why not?

♣ Collect different instruments which you could use to measure length. Draw them below.

PHOTOCOPIABLE

SCHOLASTIC
www.scholastic.co.uk

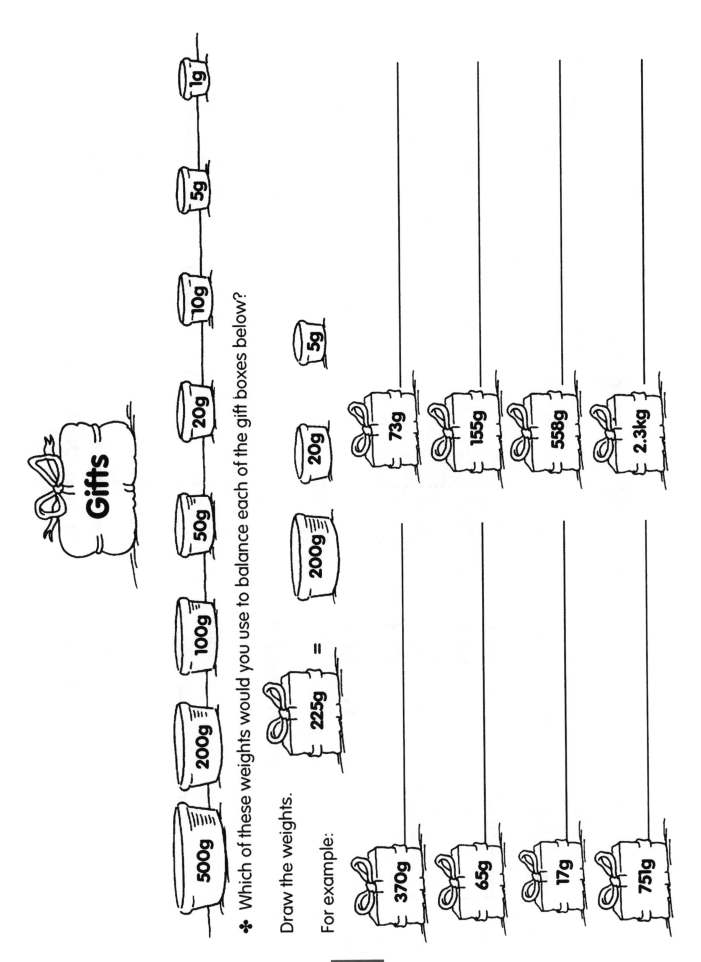

Gifts

500g 200g 100g 50g 20g 10g 5g 1g

❖ Which of these weights would you use to balance each of the gift boxes below?

Draw the weights.

For example: 225g = 200g 20g 5g

73g

155g

558g

2.3kg

370g

65g

17g

751g

📖 SCHOLASTIC
www.scholastic.co.uk

NO FUSS
PHOTOCOPIABLE

Reading a scale 1

You will need: coloured pencils.

❊ What is the volume of liquid in each of these jars?

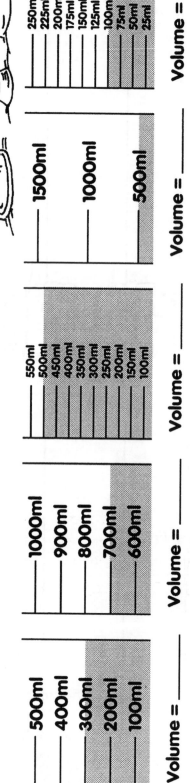

500ml	1000ml	550ml	1500ml	250ml
400ml	900ml	500ml		225ml
300ml	800ml	450ml		200ml
200ml	700ml	400ml	1000ml	175ml
100ml	600ml	350ml		150ml
		300ml		125ml
		250ml		100ml
		200ml	500ml	75ml
		150ml		50ml
		100ml		25ml

Volume = _____ Volume = _____ Volume = _____ Volume = _____ Volume = _____

❊ Complete the scales below.

300ml	125ml	180ml	850ml
	100ml	120ml	700ml
100ml		80ml	550ml
	50ml	40ml	500ml
		20ml	

Volume = 200ml Volume = 75ml Volume = 170ml Volume = 900ml

❊ Colour each jar to the level required to show the correct volume.

300ml	160ml
100ml	120ml
	100ml

Volume = 75ml Volume = 140ml

NO FUSS PHOTOCOPIABLE

Name _____

Reading a scale 2

You will need: a pencil, a collection of containers with measuring scales.

❖ Estimate the volume in each of these jars.

```
— 500ml
— 400ml
— 300ml
— 200ml
— 100ml
```

Volume = ____

```
— 2000ml
— 1500ml
— 1000ml
— 500ml
```

Volume = ____

```
— 225ml
— 200ml
— 175ml
— 150ml
— 125ml
— 100ml
— 75ml
— 50ml
— 25ml
```

Volume = ____

```
— 100ml
— 80ml
— 60ml
— 40ml
— 20ml
```

Volume = ____

```
— 370ml
— 360ml
— 350ml
— 340ml
— 330ml
```

Volume = ____

❖ Choose two of the containers used to measure volume.

❖ Draw their scales and explain what they mean.

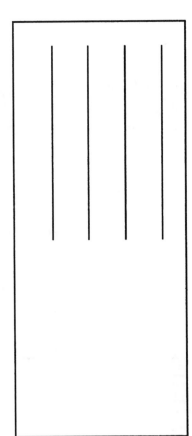

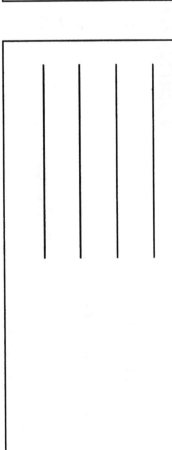

SCHOLASTIC
www.scholastic.co.uk

Telling the time

✤ Use the large clock to work out the times shown on the smaller clocks.

✤ Write the times under the clocks.

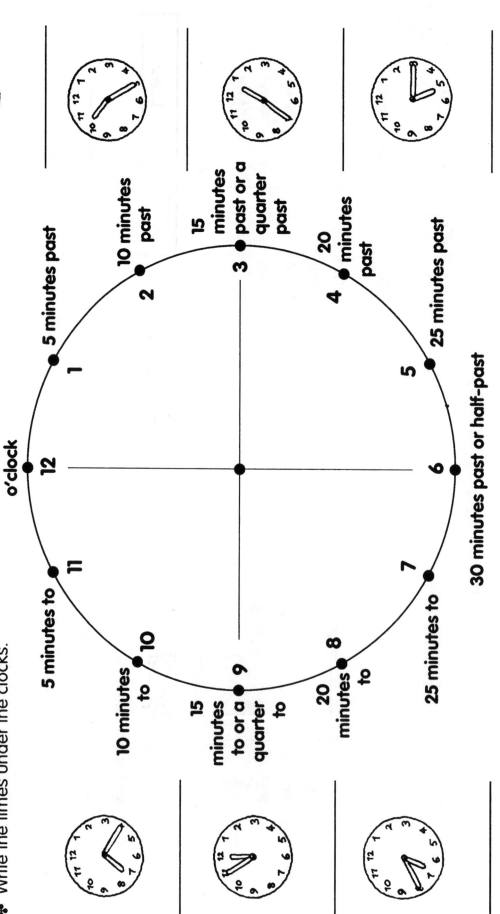

NO FUSS
PHOTOCOPIABLE

SCHOLASTIC
www.scholastic.co.uk

Name _____

On time

The display board on the right shows some of the train departure times from Central Station.

✿ As Station Master it is your job to complete the digital times next to the clocks and to answer the questions the passengers ask.

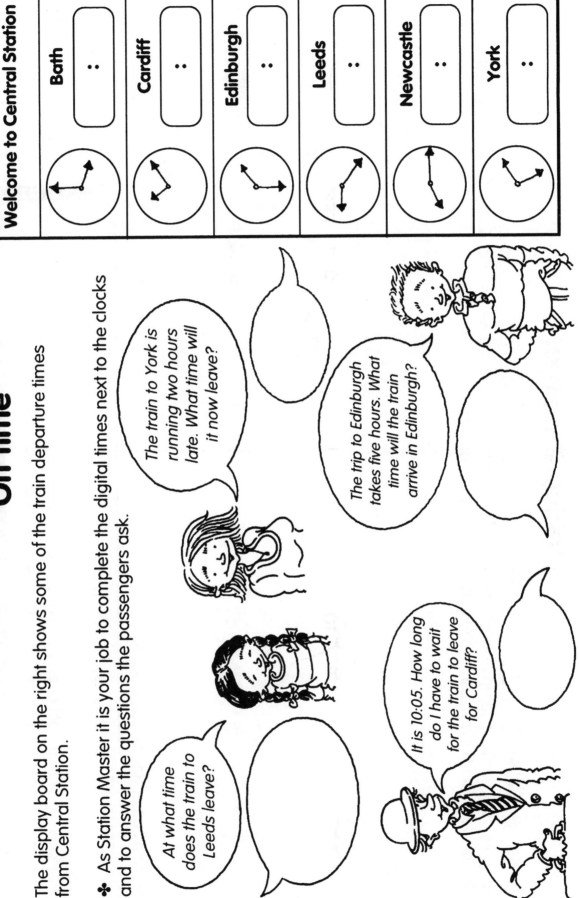

Welcome to Central Station		
Bath	∙∙	
Cardiff	∙∙	
Edinburgh	∙∙	
Leeds	∙∙	
Newcastle	∙∙	
York	∙∙	

The train to York is running two hours late. What time will it now leave?

The trip to Edinburgh takes five hours. What time will the train arrive in Edinburgh?

At what time does the train to Leeds leave?

It is 10:05. How long do I have to wait for the train to leave for Cardiff?

SCHOLASTIC
www.scholastic.co.uk

NO FUSS
PHOTOCOPIABLE

Name _____

Plasticine weights

✤ Use a 100g weight to make a lump of Plasticine that weighs 100g. Put the weight away.

✤ Now use your 100g lump of Plasticine to help you make lumps which weigh 150g, 200g, 225g, 250g and 300g.

✤ Use your Plasticine weights to weigh things in your classroom.

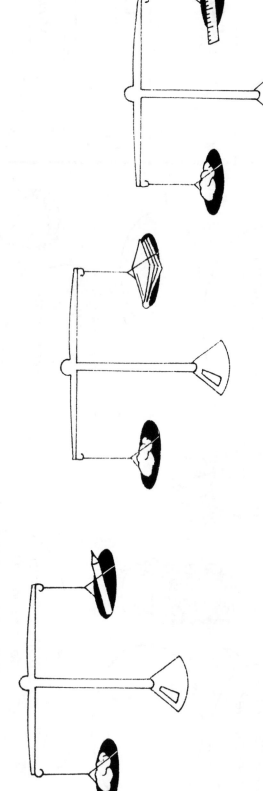

✤ Find something which weighs ...

between 100g and 200g _____
between 150g and 250g _____
between 300g and 500g _____
between 750g and 1000g _____

NO FUSS
PHOTOCOPIABLE

📖 S C H O L A S T I C
www.scholastic.co.uk

How much time?

✿ Can you write your name in less than 5 seconds? Find out.

✿ Estimate how long it would take you to write out the letters of the alphabet, then use a timing device to check your estimate.

✿ For the following activities predict, before you start, how long each activity will take you. Carry out the activity and time it. Before you check your timing device, estimate how long each activity took. Fill in the left-hand side of the chart.

✿ Now repeat the activities and fill in the right-hand side of the chart. Have your predictions and estimations become closer than in your previous attempt?

Activity to carry out	1st attempt			2nd attempt		
	Prediction of time it will take	Estimation of time it took	Time taken	Prediction of time it will take	Estimation of time it took	Time taken
Read 10 pages of a book.						
Walk around the edge of the hall.						
Run around the edge of the playground.						
Draw a picture of where you live.						
Write the names of all the people in your class.						
Throw and catch a ball 20 times.						
Say a nursery rhyme.						

■ SCHOLASTIC
www.scholastic.co.uk

Name _____

Tickets

The holders of these tickets do not know how to read 24-hour time.

✤ Explain what the 24-hour time on each one means.
Write your answers on the back of this sheet.
The first one is done for you.

McREEVIE CASTLE
ADMIT 1
Last Admission 17.15
16.10.95

BAIRD'S GARDEN PARTY
11.00 –16.30
Lunch will be served
12.30 –13.30
Cost £2.50

TASQA AIRWAYS LTD			
COOK MR C			
	CARRIER	FLIGHT	DATE	TIME
FROM				
PERTH	TQ	448	15 JUL	0600
ᵀᴼSINGAPORE	TQ	501	16 JUL	1700
ᵀᴼLONDON	VOID			

TWO-WAY BUS COMPANY
GLASGOW 17.15
to PERTH 20.22
15.10.95

CINEMA 1
ADMIT 1   20:15

FAST TRACK

From: Birmingham   10.30
To: Oxford   11.35
14.10.95   £14.95

*The train leaves Birmingham
at 10.30 in the morning and
arrives 1 hour and 5 minutes
later at 11.35.*

**ALL-DAY
ROCK CONCERT**
GATES OPEN **09.00**
GATES CLOSE **00.00**

NO FUSS
PHOTOCOPIABLE

SCHOLASTIC
www.scholastic.co.uk

Name _____

Litres and millilitres

This shopkeeper has decided that all the liquid goods in his shop must be labelled in litres.

✣ Change all the labels for him.

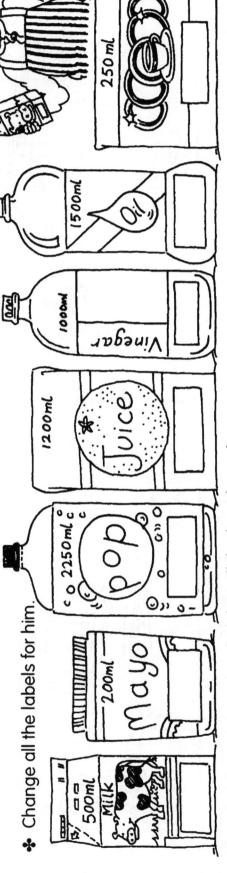

250ml

1500ml Oil

1000ml Vinegar

1200ml Juice

2250ml pop

200ml Mayo

500ml Milk

This shopkeeper has decided that all the liquid goods in her shop must be labelled in millilitres.

✣ Change all the labels for her.

0.2L Hand Lotion

2.5L Jowlene

0.1L

1l

0.5L Soap

½L WINE

¼L Beer

✣ How would you label liquids like these? _____ Why?

SCHOLASTIC
www.scholastic.co.uk

NO FUSS
PHOTOCOPIABLE

Name _____

Volume problems (cards)

Sarah has a bad cold and needs to take 10ml of medicine three times a day for five days.

800ml   75ml   175ml   100ml

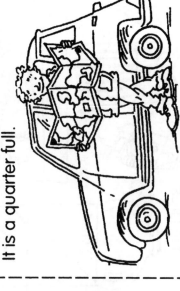

♣ Which size bottle of medicine will she need to buy?

Jan-Henrik's petrol tank holds 28l. It is a quarter full.

♣ How much petrol does he have?

Louisa and Heidi want to make a fruit punch. They are going to use 1.5l of lemonade, 900ml of cola and 500ml of orange juice.

♣ Will the punch fit in their 2.5l punchbowl?

The Walters family buy 2l of milk every day.

♣ Work out how much each person drinks if:
  Mum drinks a quarter of it.
• Morgan drinks a quarter of it.
• Greg drinks half of it.

Attila was given a 900ml bottle of bubble bath.

♣ If he uses 15ml for each bath, how many bubble baths can he have?

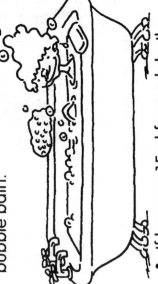

♣ How many 750ml bottles of wine could be filled from a 15l barrel?

■SCHOLASTIC
www.scholastic.co.uk

Cut ✂

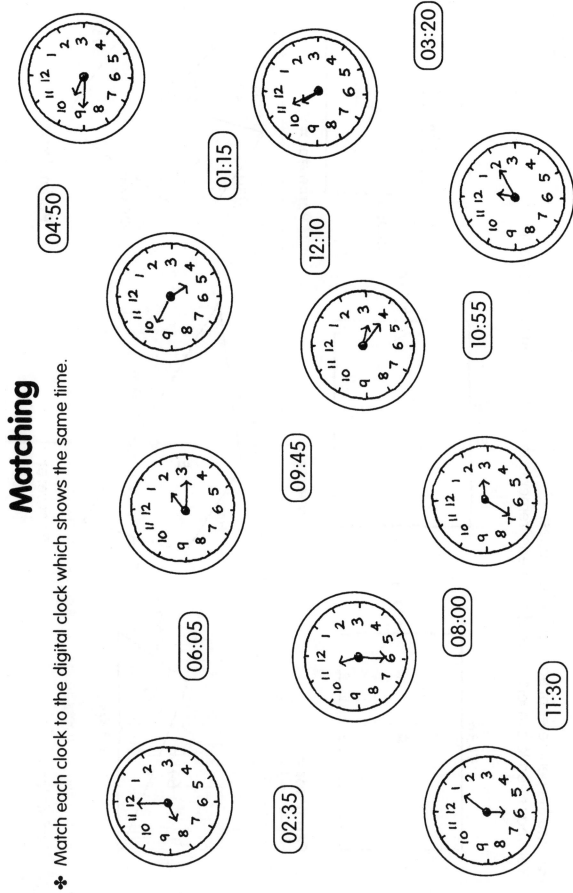

Name _____

Matching

✽ Match each clock to the digital clock which shows the same time.

■SCHOLASTIC
www.scholastic.co.uk

Name _____

Find the perimeter

♣ Find the perimeter of each of these shapes.
You may need to convert some of the measurements to a different unit before adding.

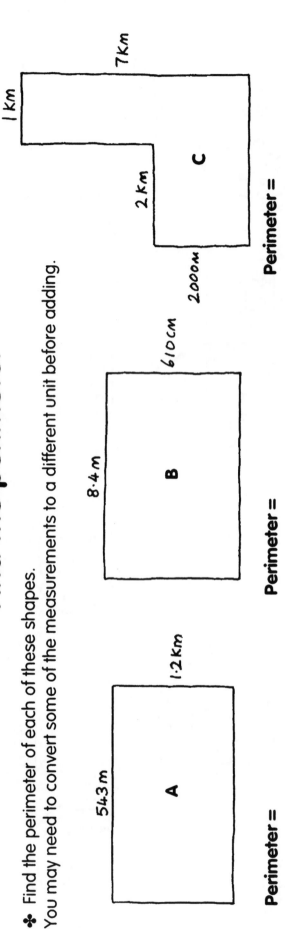

A

543 m

1·2 km

Perimeter =

B

610cm

8·4 m

Perimeter =

C

7km

1 km

2 km

2000m

Perimeter =

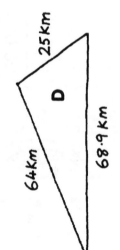

D

25 km

64 km

68·9 km

Perimeter =

E

51m

0·5km

41m

50m

Perimeter =

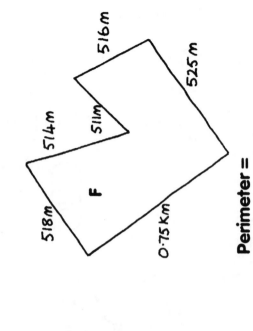

F

516m

525 m

514m

51m

518m

0·75 km

Perimeter =

NO FUSS
PHOTOCOPIABLE

SCHOLASTIC
www.scholastic.co.uk

Name _____

Circles

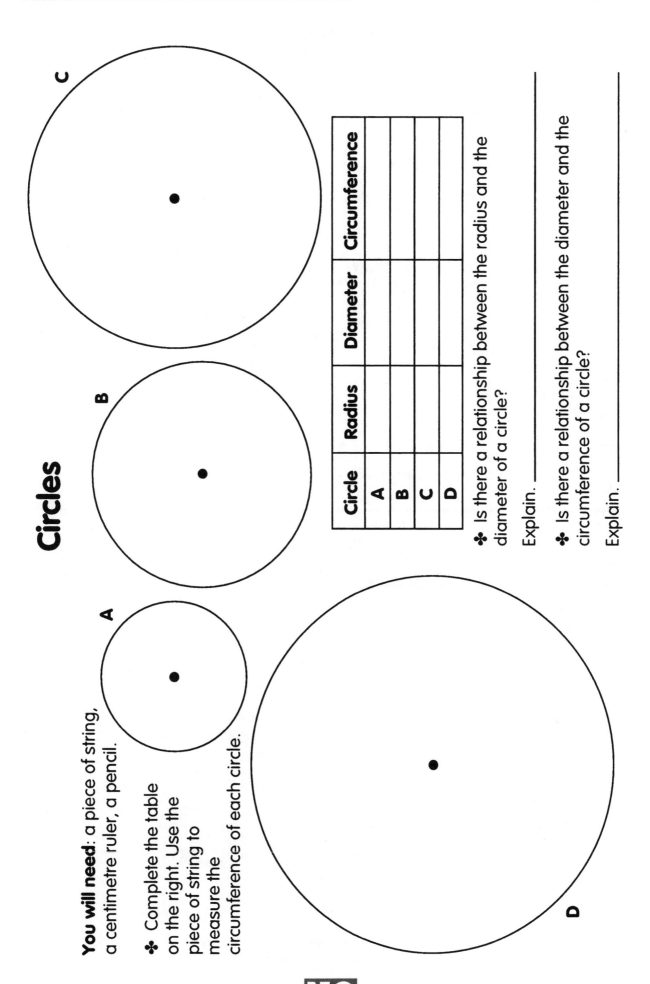

C

B

A

D

You will need: a piece of string, a centimetre ruler, a pencil.

❧ Complete the table on the right. Use the piece of string to measure the circumference of each circle.

Circle	Radius	Diameter	Circumference
A			
B			
C			
D			

❧ Is there a relationship between the radius and the diameter of a circle?

Explain. _____

❧ Is there a relationship between the diameter and the circumference of a circle?

Explain. _____

■SCHOLASTIC
www.scholastic.co.uk

NO FUSS
PHOTOCOPIABLE

SCHOLASTIC

In this series:

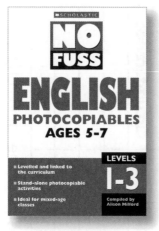

ISBN 0-439-96548-9
ISBN 978-0439-96548-4

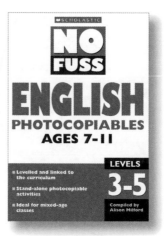

ISBN 0-439-96549-7
ISBN 978-0439-96549-1

ISBN 0-439-96550-0
ISBN 978-0439-96550-7

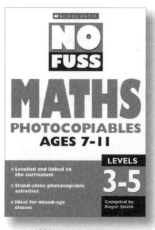

ISBN 0-439-96551-9
ISBN 978-0439-96551-4

ISBN 0-439-96552-7
ISBN 978-0439-96552-1

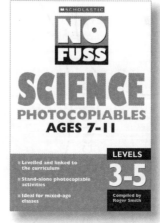

ISBN 0-439-96553-5
ISBN 978-0439-96553-8

To find out more, call: 0845 603 9091
or visit our website www.scholastic.co.uk